T0256046

Memory and Action Selection in Human–Machine Interaction

Human–Machine Interaction Set

coordinated by
Jérôme Dinet

Volume 1

Memory and Action Selection in Human–Machine Interaction

Munéo Kitajima

WILEY

First published 2016 in Great Britain and the United States by ISTE Ltd and John Wiley & Sons, Inc.

ISTE Ltd
27-37 St George's Road
London SW19 4EU
UK

www.iste.co.uk

John Wiley & Sons, Inc.
111 River Street
Hoboken, NJ 07030
USA

www.wiley.com

Library of Congress Control Number: 2015957671

British Library Cataloguing-in-Publication Data
A CIP record for this book is available from the British Library
ISBN 978-1-84821-927-4

Contents

Introduction

I.1. The key principle of designing human–machine interaction is "know the users"

"Know the users" is the key principle for designing satisfactory interactions. Users interact with information devices in order to achieve the states where they want to be. During the course of interactions, users expect a satisfactory experience. From the design side, this can be accomplished by applying the principle, "know the users", and by designing interactions accordingly to provide as much satisfaction as possible to the users through their experience of using the information devices. However, it is often hard to practice this principle due to the diversity of users. Each user has his/her own experience in using interaction devices, and his/her past experience affects significantly how he/she interacts with the devices in a particular situation. No one has the same experience. It seems there is no systematic way to practice the "know the users" principle.

"Know the users" is an important study issue not only in the field of human–machine interaction but in other domains such as behavioral economics. How does a user decide to purchase a new tablet PC for daily use? He or she selects one from a number of candidates in order to realize the states where he/she wants to be. This situation is very similar to the one described above. In the field of economics, the user's decision-making process has been studied extensively. Human decision-making is a central topic in economics. Herbert A. Simon, winner of the Nobel Prize in Economics in 1978, proposed principles of human beings' decision-making processes, the *bounded rationality principle* and the *satisficing principle* [SIM 56]. Simon claimed that agents, or human beings, face uncertainty about the future and costs when acquiring information in the present. These factors limit the extent to which human beings can make a fully rational decision, thus they possess only *bounded rationality* and must make decisions by *satisficing*, or choosing that which might not be optimal but which will make them happy enough. Recently, Kahneman [KAH 03] revealed that the core process of human beings' decision-making is an integral process of so-called *Two Minds* [EVA 09, KAH 11]. Why not consider that human brains would work similarly when people interact with information devices as when they engage in economic activities? If Two Minds is also working in human–machine interaction processes, we would be able to systematically apply the principle "know the user" for designing satisfactory interactions. A necessary condition for creating well-designed interactions is to start the design process from the consideration of how a user's brain works while he/she is interacting with the environment to be designed. In the interaction, the brain produces a series of moment-by-moment decisions concerning what to do next in the given state of the environment.

I.2. Designing human–machine interaction for Two Minds

Two Minds (see Figure I.1) refers to the following two systems: System 1, the automatic and fast unconscious decision-making process, driven by the cerebellum and oriented toward immediate action, and System 2, the deliberate and slow conscious decision-making process, driven by the cerebrum and oriented toward future action. We can easily imagine how Two Minds would work when users interact with information devices. In human–machine interactions, users deliberately consider what to do next and perform a series of actions on the device automatically. At the same time, they pay attention to the device's feedback and plan future actions accordingly. What we need to understand is how users switch between the slow and the fast processes of Two Minds, and explain and predict the behaviors we observe. The users' behaviors change depending on how the interaction is designed. The smoother the switching, the more the users would feel satisfaction. By taking the interaction between the slow deliberate processes and the fast automatic processes explicitly into account, we will be able to design interactions that are likely to satisfy the users' interaction experience.

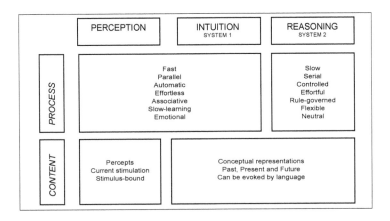

Figure I.1. *Process and Content in Two Cognitive Systems (adapted from [KAH 03])*

However, it will not be an easy task because there is a huge difference in processing speed between the two systems; rational processing with System 2 typically takes minutes to hours, whereas experiential processing with System 1 typically extends from hundreds of milliseconds to tens of seconds [NEW 90]. A large part of human beings' daily activities are immediate actions and are therefore under the control of System 1. System 2 intervenes with System 1 to better organize the overall outcome of the processing through consciously envisioning possible futures.

What does it mean for the interaction design activities of Two Minds to rely on people's behaviors? I would like to suggest that interaction design is about designing time for the user in terms of a series of events that the user will be provided at a specific time T, by taking into account the fact that the user's process is controlled by Two Minds. This is because interactions take place at the interface of a system and a user, and the only dimension that the system and the user's Two Minds can share is the time dimension. The user decides what to do next by using his/her Two Minds at time $T - \alpha$, carries it out at time T, the system responds to it at $T + \beta$ and this cycle continues. The system's response at $T + \beta$ needs to take into account how the user's Two Minds would process it. He/she may expect the system's response for consciously confirming or unconsciously matching whether he/she did right or not, or he/she may expect it for consciously planning or unconsciously triggering the next action. The user's expectations can become diverse but interaction designers need to take them into account appropriately in order for the designed system to satisfy the users' expectations.

Here is an example to illustrate this point. When we hear a car navigation system speaking in synthesized voice, we switch our attention to what it says and try to plan our driving for the near future. The navigation system is designed to speak, for example, "slight right turn in point five miles on South Lynn Street", with the screenshot shown in Figure I.2 at some specific moment. The driver, who is not familiar with the route, is supposed to listen to the instructions and read the screen carefully, integrating the information provided from the car navigation system with the current driving situation, imagining and planning the immediate-future driving and creating a sequence of actions for the maneuver: when to start reducing speed, when to start braking and so forth. When the navigation system starts speaking at time T, "slight right turn ...", it should affect the driver's on-going processes and initiate a new interactive process stream on the part of the driver.

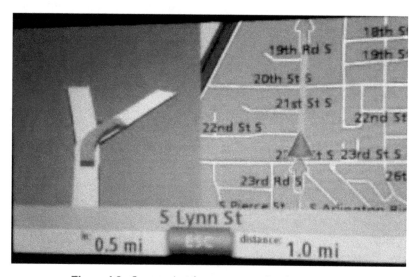

Figure I.2. *Screenshot from a car navigation system*

This interaction must be designed well by taking into account whatever Two Minds processes the driver engages in so that the newly initiated process does not interfere with other on-going processes; some processes must be suspended and resumed at an appropriate time (with little cost), and other processes can continue with no interference from the car navigation system (e.g. keep conversing with a person in the passenger seat).

I.3. Organization of the book

This book is organized in two parts, one part theory and another part practice.

I.3.1. *Theoretical foundation for dealing with action selection and memorization as a cyclic nonlinear process*

The first goal of this book is to extend Two Minds from its origins in behavioral economics to the domain of interaction, where the time dimension has to be dealt with rigorously; in the human–machine interaction (HMI), establishing synchronization between conscious processes and unconscious processes is crucial for the feeling of smoothness, as is the way in which memory processes and action selection processes are coordinated. The first half of the book describes the theory in detail. Chapter 1 outlines the whole view of the theory, consisting of action selection processes and memorization processes and their interactions. Chapter 2 provides a detailed description for action selection processes theorized as a nonlinear dynamic human behavior model with real-time constraints, followed by Chapter 3, which provides a detailed description for memorization processes. As the final section of the theory part, Chapter 4 discusses implications of the theory to HMIs. The most important point to understand human behavior in the ever-changing environment is that human behavior is regarded as a cycle of action selection and memorization processes that begin at one's birth and ends at one's death. In addition, action selection is carried out through a multilayered structure, with characteristic times, and a multilayered memory structure, and therefore the processes that control human behavior have to be treated as the result of nonlinear processes. Nonlinearity, or complex system, implies sensitive dependence on initial condition (SEDIC), i.e. a small variation in the initial condition, during one's infant period, develops exponentially as one grows up. Therefore, human behavior as observed in the current environment should be regarded as the result of adaptation to the current ecological environment and his/her memory that has been constructed through his/her behavioral experience that has been accumulated at the time of action selection. Action selection is carried out either by selecting or recalling one from existing memory, or searching for an appropriate one for the current situation. However, this is not predictable as in a linear system since action selection is carried out in a complex system. This is summarized as follows:

Dynamic phenomena in a complex system

=

Structure constructed in a cyclic complex system

×

Environmental variation in a cyclic complex system

I.3.2. *Theoretically motivated methodology for understanding users*

The second goal of this book is to provide a methodology to study how Two Minds works in practice when people use interactive systems. How does Two Minds work in HMI? What is the user's performance under Two Minds? It has been proposed by Edwin Hutchins by the name of "cognitive ethnography" (CE). However, the most important thing to be understood is how the fast unconscious process and the slow deliberate process work together to create a series of decision-making events concerning what to do next and generate coherent behavior, i.e. the dynamics of Two Minds working in the ever-changing environment. The dynamics is best defined by using the time dimension explicitly. The second half of this book describes the practical aspect of the theory in detail. Chapter 5 introduces a new methodology called cognitive chrono-ethnography (CCE), which adds the time dimension to Hutchins' CE in order to practice "know the users" systematically by designing user studies based on a simulation of users' mental operations controlled by Two Minds. Chapters 6 and 7 show how CCE has been applied to understand how people navigate in real physical environments by walking and by car, respectively. As the final section of the practice part, Chapter 8 explores the possibility of applying CCE to predict people's future needs. This is not meant for understanding how people use interfaces at present but for predicting how people will want to use interfaces in the future given how they are currently using them.

I.3.3. *Conditions for sustainable HMI*

Finally, this book concludes by describing the implications of HMIs that are carried out while using modern artifacts for people's cognitive development from their births on the basis of the theories of action selection and memorization described.

PART 1

Theoretical Foundation for Dealing with Action Selection and Memorization

A Unified Theory of Action Selection and Memory

The purpose of this chapter is to provide a bird's-eye view of our project[1], the development of a framework for considering the behavior of human beings in the universe, nonlinear dynamic human behavior model with real-time constraints (NDHB-model/RT), and a cognitive architecture, "model human processor with real-time constraints" (MHP/RT), that is capable of simulating human being's daily decision making and action selection under NDHB-model/RT. The underlying idea is discussed in section 1.1.

1.1. Organic self-consistent field theory

1.1.1. *Self-consistent field theory in physics*

In physics and probability theory, self-consistent field theory (SCFT), also known as mean field theory, studies the behavior of large and complex stochastic models by studying a simpler model. Such models consider a large number of small interacting individual components, which interact with each other. The effect of all other individuals on any given individual is approximated by a single averaged effect, thus reducing a many-body problem to a one-body problem. In field theory, the Hamiltonian may be expanded in terms of the magnitude of fluctuations around the mean of the

---

1 The work discussed in this book is the result of a decade of collaboration between Makoto Toyota, cognitive architect, and Munéo Kitajima, cognitive scientist, the author of this book. The author is deeply grateful to Matkoto Toyota for his distinguished talent as a cognitive architect to imagine the complex working of the human brain. Throughout this book, "we" refers to "Makoto Toyota and Munéo Kitajima" unless it clearly implies people in general.

field. In this context, SCFT can be viewed as the "zeroth-order" expansion of the Hamiltonian in fluctuations. In reality, this means an SCFT system has no fluctuations, but this coincides with the idea that one is replacing all interactions with a "self-consistent field". Quite often, in the formalism of fluctuations, SCFT provides a convenient launch point to study first- or second-order fluctuations.

1.1.2. *"Organic" SCFT*

We applied SCFT in physics to organic systems. Organic systems are those composed of human beings as their components. Any organic system can be represented as a model that considers a large number of individual human beings which interact with each other. In addition, individual "organic" human beings interact with "inorganic" physical environments as well, which is also modeled by SCFT. We prefixed the word "organic" to SCFT in order to explicitly indicate that the application domain of SCFT is extended to organic systems. We consider that the behavior of human beings in the universe is quasi-stable, which means that it is not stable but develops or evolves as a result of some fluctuations, a feature of the dissipative system – a fluctuation of the system caused by an environmental change could trigger the creation of a new order or catastrophe [PRI 85].

1.1.3. *Human beings considered in O-SCFT*

At the zeroth-order approximation implied by organic SCFT (O-SCFT), each human being interacts with the integrated environment consisting of inorganic components and organic components. Each human being is considered as *an autonomous system*, and interaction is best represented by *information flow* from the viewpoint of human being. Figure 1.1 shows the following three nonlinear constructs for representing human beings in O-SCFT:

1) Maximum satisfaction architecture (MSA) is about realization of the purpose of living, *libido* – it maximizes efforts on the autonomous system, i.e. each human being. It deals with how autonomous systems achieve goals under constraints defined by brain information hydrodynamics (BIH) and structured meme theory (SMT) [KIT 07], to be explained in what follows.

2) Brain information hydrodynamics (BIH) represents the constraints from the environment, which correspond to inorganic SCFT components. It defines how the information flow develops along the time dimension in the brain of individual human being [KIT 08].

3) Structured meme theory (SMT) represents the relational structure that links human beings, MSA, and the environment, inorganic SCF, to construct organic SCF. SMT concerns effective information and the range of propagation of information [TOY 08].

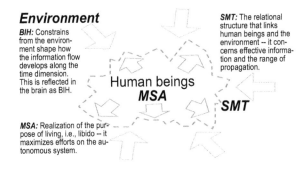

Figure 1.1. *Three fundamental constructs of O-SCFT*

1.1.4. *Scale mix*

Organic self-consistent field (SMT) provides a rather macroscopic viewpoint and considers the system in question as stable and obeys the law of increase in entropy (second law of thermodynamics), whereas BIH, corresponding to inorganic self-consistent field, provides a rather microscopic viewpoint where the universe is essentially a dissipative structure of a complex system that self-organizes as a hierarchical structure [PRI 85].

Gaia, the environment of the earth as a whole, is an extremely developed world with a complex hierarchical structure. Any phenomena in Gaia appear as the results of scale-mixed compounds of individual phenomena that coexist at different hierarchies characterized by their own scales in time and space. Any entities in the complex hierarchical structure that live across the multiple hierarchies should exist under a certain balance in the scale mix. Therefore, understanding human beings who live under MSA can be achieved by considering their lives in a certain balance between organic self-consistent field, SMT, and inorganic self-consistent filed, BIH, established as a hierarchical structure.

1.2. Development of brain architecture model under the NDHB model/RT

We are not only interested in how individual human beings' brains process information, originated either from external or internal environment, but also by how it develops from his/her birth. We challenge this problem under the concept of MSA, BIH and SMT.

1.2.1. *O-PDP*

We focus on information flow in the brain. We considered that *parallel distributed processing* (PDP) is the fundamental mechanism for developing brain architecture [MCC 87]. Since PDP is considered under O-SCFT, we prefixed "O (organic)" to PDP, O-PDP, to indicate it explicitly.

O-PDP develops cross-networks of neurons in the brain as it accumulates experience of interactions in the environment. *The neural network development process is circular*, which means that any experience at a particular moment should somehow reflect the experience of past interactions that have been recorded in the shape of current neural networks. In this way, a PDP system is organized evolutionally and realized as a neural network system including the brain, the spinal nerves and the peripheral nerves.

1.2.2. *The guideline for architecture selection*

O-PDP represents the working of the entire organic system as a whole, in which a number of autonomous systems function in the ever-changing real environment. The strong constraint is that O-PDP evolves over time for millions of years in the largest scope, and develops from one's birth in the one-generation scope in the environment of Gaia. It is likely that a number of architectures could explain the behavior of human beings in the current status of Gaia. However, we aimed at constructing one that should be consistent with the evolution history of human beings as well. This is the guideline we adopted for constructing our architecture. Figure 1.2 depicts this schematically. It is quite reasonable to consider this as the optimum solution that resides at the intersection of the trace of evolution of human beings and the system architectures that are capable of reproducing the characteristics of current human beings.

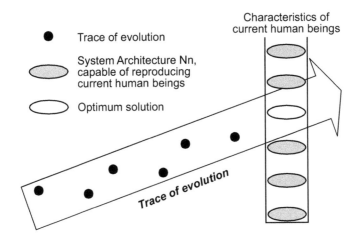

Figure 1.2. *The guideline we adopted for selecting our architecture*

1.2.3. *Development of cross-networks of neurons in the brain*

As Swanson [SWA 11] explains, cross-networks of neurons in the brain develop in a systematic way to show the three-layered structure of the interneurons system (Figure 1.3). Interneurons intervene in the sensory nervous system that is responsible for processing sensory information and in the somatic nervous system that is associated with the voluntary control of body movements via skeletal muscles to form a complex paired structure of perception and motion. They consist of direct feed-forward connections from perception to motion, and more complex connections with feedback loops using the interneurons to form three distinguishable layers.

Body movement is constructed by selecting executable motions and sequencing them in such a way that it adapts to the current environmental constraints. A motion is executable when it is exerted with stable postures, which are realized as a musculoskeletal system that has been formed via the developmental and experiential processes according to the deoxyribonucleic acid (DNA) body plan. A body movement could be associated with multiple different purposes. Therefore, meaning to particular body movement is given *consciously* as a compound social ecology. In this way, PDP by McClelland and Rumelhart [MCC 87] is naturally integrated with evolutional view described by Swanson [SWA 11].

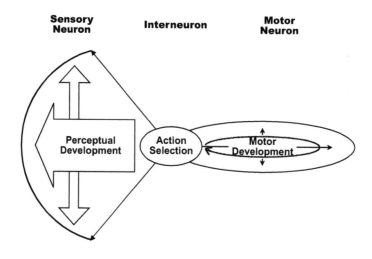

Figure 1.3. *Development of the sensory nervous system and the somatic nervous system, and interneurons connecting them with the action selection process (adapted from [KIT 15a])*

According to Damasio [DAM 99], a vertebrate animal develops its neural network system in the following way. It starts with the development of the paired structure consisting of the sense of touch and reflexive movements associated with it. Then, the sense of smell and the sense of taste, and, finally, the sense of seeing and the sense of hearing develop their associations with reflexive movements. From the beginning, the perceptual stimuli from the five senses form a paired structure with their associated reflexive movements. In addition, the association tends to become bidirectional for the purpose of establishing selective sensing, which is a paired structure with feedback between perception and movement. For example, the sense of hearing and the sense of vocalization establish a feedback loop between them immediately after one acquires the function of voicing.

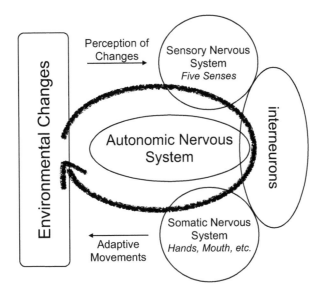

Figure 1.4. *Continuous cyclic loop of perception and movement (adapted from [KIT 14a])*

The neural network system forms at first the autonomic nervous system of respective autonomous organs as a genetic fundamental structure, then crosses it with the somatic nervous system that controls reflexive movements associated with the perceptual stimuli from the five senses, and develops the feedback loops with a system of interneurons that connect these systems. Figure 1.4 depicts this loop schematically.

Pushing this further, we have developed the NDHB-model/RT (see Chapter 2) as an architecture model that consists of a number of autonomous systems including the perceptual system, conscious system (System 2), unconscious system (System 1), memory system, behavior control system, and so on. A number of theories have been constructed as the project develops. Respective theories take different viewpoints for observing a variety of phenomena generated by the single mechanism of O-PDP.

2

NDHB-Model/RT: Nonlinear Dynamic Human Behavior Model with Realtime Constraints

The purpose of this chapter is to integrate the three fundamental constructs of O-SCFT (MSA, BIH and SMT), briefly introduced in Chapter 1, into a unity. The following sections provide more detailed explanations of the fundamental constructs, then define the Nonlinear Dynamic Human Behavior Model with Realtime Constraints (NDHB-model/RT).

2.1. Maximum satisfaction architecture

As described in section 1.1.3, MSA is about the realization of the purpose of living, libido – it maximizes efforts on the autonomous system. It deals with how autonomous systems achieve goals under constraints defined by BIH and SMT [KIT 07].

MSA consists of the following three parts:

1) happiness goals, i.e. basic living purposes of human beings;

2) human brain;

3) society.

2.1.1. Happiness goals

MSA assumes that the human brain pursues one of the 17 happiness goals defined by Morris [MOR 06] at every moment, and switches when appropriate by evaluating the current circumstances. Table 2.1 lists each of the happiness goals along with the name of type associated with it, and describe their relationships to social layers.

	Happiness	Types	Individual level	Community level	Social system level
1	Target happiness	The achiever	+++	+++	+++
2	Competitive happiness	The winner		+++	+++
3	Cooperative happiness	The helper		+++	+++
4	Genetic happiness	The relative	+++	+++	
5	Sensual happiness	The hedonist	+++	+++	
6	Cerebral happiness	The intellectual	+++	+++	++
7	Rhythmic happiness	The dancer	+++	+++	
8	Painful happiness	The masochist	+++		
9	Dangerous happiness	The risk taker	+++	++	+
10	Selective happiness	The hysteric	+++	++	
11	Tranquil happiness	The mediator	+++		
12	Devout happiness	The believer		+++	++
13	Negative happiness	The suffer	+++	++	
14	Chemical happiness	The drug taker	+++		
15	Fantasy happiness	The daydreamer	+++		
16	Comic happiness	The laugher	+++	+++	
17	Accidental happiness	The fortunate	+++	+++	+++

Table 2.1. *Happiness goals and their relation to social layers. + denotes the degree of relevance of each goal to each layer, i.e. Individual, Community, and Social system, respectively. +++: most relevant, ++: moderately relevant, and +: weakly relevant*

2.1.2. *Society layers*

Each of the happiness goals is associated with one or more layers of society: individual, family and community, and administration and enterprise. These layers have evolved from the history of human beings. Each layer is associated with its own value reflecting historical development, and thus different sets of happiness goals are relevant.

2.1.3. *Brain layers*

The knowledge necessary to achieve the happiness goals is partly acquired and partly inherited, which is stored in three brain layers[1]. At the level of the

---

1 As will be introduced in section 2.2.3 where BIH is described in detail, the brain consists of three layers: conscious state layer, autonomous-automatic behavior control layer and bodily state layer.

conscious state layer, knowledge, such as formal laws and social mechanisms necessary to deal with administration and enterprise, and formal social norms and common sense to deal with "family and community" and "individual", is acquired. In contrast, knowledge such as basic functions for using language and primitive decision characteristics is inherited. Similarly, at the level of autonomous-automatic behavior control layer, knowledge such as individual experience and habit is acquired to deal with "family and community" and "individual". However, as opposed to the inherited knowledge at the conscious state layer, all basic functions that are reproducible by the development and bodily experience are inherited in the autonomous-automatic behavior control layer.

Figure 2.1 depicts the entire relationships among happiness goals, society layers and brain layers. At every moment, an organism tries to achieve one of the happiness goals. Each happiness goal is associated with the nonlinear three-layered structure of society. The goal is achieved by using the nonlinear three-layered structure of brain: whose detail has been affected by the nonlinear three-layered structure of society on the one hand, and whose detail would impose strong constraints on how the goal is accomplished in the ever-changing environment on the other hand. It is assumed that by accomplishing the goal, the organism experiences satisfaction. The individual layers in society and in the brain are mutually related. The mechanism is complicated, but in order to understand human beings' behavior in the ever-changing world, it is extremely needed to consider the relationships among happiness goals, society and the brain, not independently but as a whole entity.

In addition, the pieces of knowledge at each layer in the brain and the society are nonlinearly interconnected through individual experience. Nonlinearity means two important things that affect development of an individual's brain–society system:

   – *Dissipative system*: a fluctuation of the system caused by an environmental change would trigger creation of a new order or catastrophe;

   – *Sensitive dependence on initial condition (SEDIC)*: a small variation in the initial condition during one's infant period would develop exponentially as one grows up.

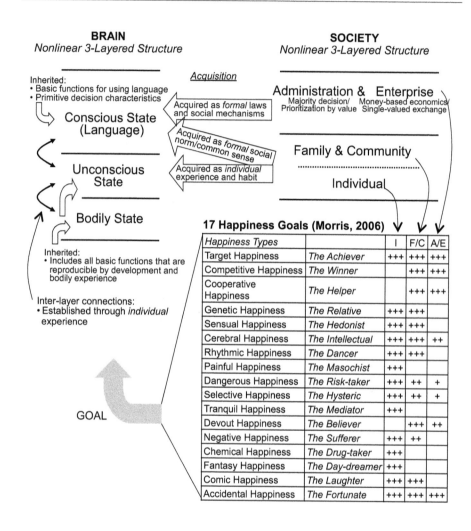

Figure 2.1. *Maximum satisfaction architecture (MSA)*

This implies that individuals that pursue the same goal might have different patterns of activated networks because of SEDIC, and thus the processes to achieve the goal might be different. An intelligent autonomous agent incorporated with human–machine interactions must be sensitive to the individual differences in the processes to achieve a goal and provide sophisticated support for individuals to achieve that goal. This has a deep implication to the main theme of this book "know the users", because this provides an important hint for the way in which to conduct "know the users" endeavors.

2.1.4. *Conditions to make people feel satisfaction*

The amount of satisfaction felt by a user is influenced by the factors that characterize the shape of trajectory of behavioral outcome. There are six critical factors to make people feel satisfaction (see Figure 2.2).

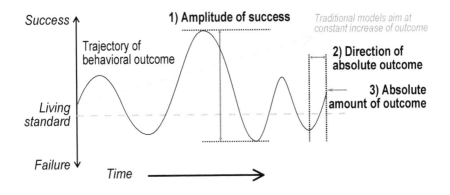

Figure 2.2. *Conditions to make people feel satisfaction*

1) *Change*: perceptual functions work by sensing dynamic changes. Therefore, responses while the system is stable are limited. A condition for feeling satisfaction is "change";

2) *Succession of good results:* successive happiness tends to create memory traces for the best experience and the final outcome of the overall estimation of the events that have lead to successive good results;

3) *Direction of absolute outcome (denoted as 2 in Figure 2.2)*: a change to good direction at the end of a series of events tends to create a memory trace of having felt satisfaction. The degree of the strength of the memory trace would be proportional to the degree of the change toward good direction;

4) *Amplitude of success (denoted as 1 in Figure 2.2)*: the greater the difference between the highest event and the lowest event in terms of the degree of the strength of satisfactory feeling, the stronger the strength of a memory

trace for the entire events, including the highest and the lowest. We create feelings of satisfaction as a result of overcoming the lowest evaluated situation and also tend to memorize these;

5) *Absolute amount of outcome (denoted as 3 in Figure 2.2) and direction of absolute outcome (denoted as 2 in Figure 2.2)*: when the absolute outcome is acceptable and the contents in working memory at the time of final event are good, they jointly affect the result of estimation of entire events;

6) *Bad results would not be memorized*: when an event occurs that results in bad results, we strongly react to it if the degree of badness exceeds a certain threshold value. This event creates a memory trace for a must-avoid event. However, memory traces for events that are exerted while recovering from the bad situation tend to be weak because conscious processes work in their full performance.

2.2. Brain information hydrodynamics

Constraints from the environment shape how the flow of information develops along the time dimension. This is reflected in the brain as BIH. It deals with information flow in the brain and its characteristics in time [KIT 08]. At present, there is no research method for viewing the brain from a broad perspective. We suggest that theories of complex systems such as fluid are useful. We therefore propose BIH as a theory that should serve as a basis for constructing a unified theory of action selection and memory, which is traditionally conceived as an electronically based neuronal network and/or chemically based hormone field. In BIH, the influx of information from the environment is filtered at the entrance of the brain to reduce the amount of information to a tractable number of chunks. The influx flows along the terrain, which was originally shaped by genes and then transformed through experience. Immediate behavior is generated when the influx reaches the cerebellum directly. Deliberate behavior, i.e. the outcome of the cerebrum, is generated when the influx is trapped midway to the cerebellum where a number of vortices are created to transform the values of attributes of the information that the influx conveys successively to the ones finally exerted. The real-time constraint of behavior is satisfied by creating emotional vortices, as will be described in section 2.2.4 in detail, that force the flow to reach the cerebellum in a timely manner.

BIH deals with *information flow* in the brain, as shown in Figure 2.1, as a nonlinear three-layered structure and its characteristics in the time dimension. Biological activity can be viewed as the results of information flow in the brain and it shows the characteristics of complex systems and dissipative structure. In other words, it is best characterized by *hydrodynamics* at the microscopic phenomenological level and by *thermodynamics* at the macroscopic collective level. Table 2.2 summarizes the features of the theories.

	Characteristics	Theory
Macroscopic level	Collective	Thermodynamics
Microscopic level	Phenomenological	Hydrodynamics

Table 2.2. *Biological Activity: Complex Systems and Dissipative Structure*

2.2.1. The time axis is central to information flow

Time is the fourth dimension of our four-dimensional physical universe. However, unlike the *X*, *Y* and *Z* dimensions, it is not symmetric; in other words, it is not reversible. The order of our universe is being shaped as the interactions between life and the surrounding environment and develops along the one-directional time dimension. The characteristic times of brain information processing ensure sustainability of those interactions.

The functioning brain is the result of the working of a huge network of 20 billion nerve cells and synapses. It basically converts input signals from the environment to information that is necessary for acting in real time. However, the phenomena that the flow of information in the brain causes are extraordinarily complex. We suggest that this is analogous to the complexity of the phenomena exhibited by a flow of fluid and that it is useful to apply the construct of the theory of hydrodynamics metaphorically to the phenomena of information flow in the brain.

2.2.2. Cerebrum formation process

In the very early days, organisms created cerebellum-like feed-forward networks, as shown in Figure 2.3. They were most suitable for generating prompt responses to the occurrence of libido, which is the free creative energy an individual has to apply to personal development. Those networks enabled the organisms to perform the required sequence of actions very smoothly: collecting information from the external environment, taking actions for satisfying the occurring libido, achieving it and, finally, returning to the resting state.

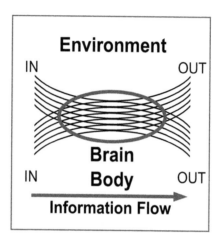

Figure 2.3. *Interaction between brain and environment based on feed-forward control*

After developing the cerebellum-like feed-forward networks, organisms then developed the cerebrum. As opposed to cerebellum, the cerebrum is equipped with feedback networks for processing information as shown in Figure 2.4. These networks enabled the organisms to perform complicated information processing that was impossible for cerebellum-like feed-forward networks.

How have the feedback networks developed from the feed-forward networks? Here is our answer. When libido occurs, information from the external environment is gathered via sensory organs, eyes for visual information, nose for olfactory information and ears for auditory information. The set of information originating from the variety of sensors with different modalities constitutes a set of information flows in the brain network. They flow simultaneously and quasi-independently, and are ultimately transformed into the information for generating external actions.

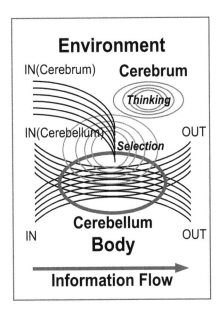

Figure 2.4. *Formation of cerebrum*

However, the pattern of the flows is very complex because individual flows are not synchronous in time but the set of flows must converge at the time when an action associated with the input is taken. The timing of action is strictly determined by *real-time constraints*. Some flows may have spare time and have to wait until the other flows are ready to be integrated, or synchronized. While waiting, the flows of information may develop an order that is analogous to vortices in the stream of river. In the brain network, informational vortices may develop, drift, disappear, fission and merge. A vortex can interact with the other vortices. These vortices can be conceived as manifestation of some functions that work as part of feedback control.

2.2.3. Information flows in the brain

The brain consists of three nonlinearly connected layers as its structure and functions enabled by activating part of the structure.

– *C layer*: conscious state layer, including basic functions for using language and primitive decision characteristics, is acquired as formal laws and social mechanisms, and as formal social norms and common sense (the top layer of BRAIN as shown in Figure 2.1);

– A^2BC *layer*: autonomous-automatic behavior control layer is acquired as individual experience and habit (the middle layer of BRAIN as shown in Figure 2.1);

– *B layer*: bodily state layer includes all basic functions that are reproduced by development and bodily experience (the bottom layer of BRAIN as shown in Figure 2.1).

Note that basic functions working at the C layer and B layer are inherited from the predecessors. Interlayer connections between the C layer and A^2BC layer, and between the A^2BC layer and B layer are established through individual experience, which should be different individual by individual and SEDIC should apply.

2.2.4. *Emergence of emotion in BIH*

Information flows in each layer with its specific purpose as shown by Figure 2.5. In the C layer, information is for predicting the time course of events and for coordinating relationships between the self and others. In the A^2BC layer, information is for autonomously and automatically controlling a variety of parts of the body. In the B layer, information is for regulating the bodily state.

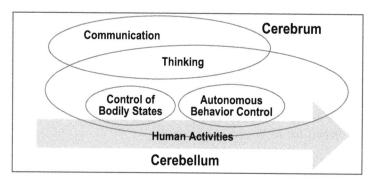

Figure 2.5. *Information flows in the brain*

Vortices emerge in a river when the amount of flow exceeds a certain threshold. Similarly, when the amount of information flow in the brain exceeds its threshold, informational vortices emerge in the network. These vortices correspond to some conscious states.

In BIH, emotions are regarded as the phenomena by which the information flows in the three layers are interrupted in order to take timely actions; in other words, the real-time constraints intervene in the information flows that may not converge and synchronize at the time an action must be taken. The vortices collapse immediately, i.e. conscious thinking terminates in favor of taking timely action.

2.2.5. Biorhythm of information flow

Information flow in the brain has a 1-day cycle. While sleeping, the amount of the flow stays at a minimum level. In the daytime, the flow increases to the maximum level while working intensively. However, the actual amount of flow is determined by the relationships between the state of the external environment and the desire of the self. Metaphorically, the 1-day cycle of information flow is similar to the daily changes in the ebb and flow in a narrow strait where the emergence of vortices depends on the amount of the one-directional tidal stream.

2.2.6. Role of language

The vortices emerge spontaneously when conditions are satisfied. However, as the skill of using language develops, matures and begins to be stably inherited among generations, it starts to work as a trigger for the appearance of vortices, such as pegs which cause turbulent flows that make vortices emerge.

2.2.7. Multiple personality disorder

When making decisions, a number of candidate actions are evaluated for their suitability in the current situation. However, the actions that are actually taken are largely determined by the evaluation performed by the experience-based reward system located at the junction of the cerebrum and the cerebellum. This evaluation process is unconscious.

In the human brain, there naturally coexist multiple personalities. In the cerebrum, there are a number of small-scale networks that serve as elements for defining personality. The combination of the partial elements, which is the result of information flow in the cerebrum, is determined by the reward system, and therefore there is the possibility of emergence of one personality for some situation and another for a different situation. Personality emergence depends solely on the external information that is fed to the brain, the contingency of selection of the route of information flow in the cerebrum, and the nature of the experience-based reward system.

2.3. Structured meme theory

SMT concerns the relational structure that links human beings and the environment, and thereby deals with effective information and the range of propagation [TOY 08]. The recent consensus is that the range of informational inheritance by genes is limited to physical functions and infantile behavior. Human beings need to acquire basic behavioral skills and communicational skills through experience of behaving in the environment. We propose SMT that explains acquisition and development of these skills. SMT consists of action-, behavior- and culture-level memes. These are interconnected nonlinearly and reflect the level of complexity of brain functions that map information in the environment onto internal representations. The mechanism with which the three levels of memes and genes inherit information is analogous to an information system. Genes serve as firmware that mimics behavior-level activities. Action-level memes serve as the operating system that defines general patterns of spatial–temporal behavioral functions. Behavior-level memes serve as middleware that extends the general patterns to concrete patterns. Culture-level memes serve as application tools that extend the concrete patterns to the ones that work in a number of groups of people.

2.3.1. Meme

A meme is an entity that represents the information associated with the object that the brain can recognize. The original term "meme" coined by Dawkins in 1970s [DAW 76] was conceptual and not clearly defined. However, the meme, or the structured meme, in SMT proposed in this paper is defined clearly within the framework of a nonlinear, multilayered information structure that is similar to the structure of living organisms.

A meme is defined as follows. Each object is defined as a set of elements that belong to each layer in a nonlinearly connected multilayered structure. Those elements that are recognizable as proper entities, such as shape, movement and quality, are able to exist as memes (latent memes). These latent memes change to manifest memes when they are fixated as a part of an object or memorized by the other persons as information objects through the experience that the self takes part in. As such, memes exist in the brain not only as entities that correspond to real objects that exist in the environment but also as information objects that are included in the layers the elements of the objects belong to. For human beings, the latter has been constructed by mapping environmental information onto the networks in the brain, which has established the relationships between human beings and their surrounding environment. This explains the emergence of cultural differences among living groups.

The structured meme consists of the following three nonlinear layers:

– action-level memes represent bodily actions;

– behavior-level memes represent behaviors in the environment;

– culture-level memes represent culture.

Memes as a whole are a collection of information objects that reside in each layer. Each person will develop his/her own relationships among objects.

Figure 2.6 depicts the structure of inheritance of information in which genes, memes, and language participate.

2.3.2. *Memes propagate by means of resonance*

Memes propagate from person to person when the receiver estimates that the degree of reality of the meme perceived by him/her reaches a certain level. The process of feeling reality can be conceived as the process of resonance that occurs in the brain in response to the input of memes from a sender. When the meme in question resonates with some patterns associated with valued experiences endorsed by the reward system, the meme is accepted by the receiver. The entire meme structure in human society is a networked field defined by individuals' connections. Each person's brain forms a proper reality field, and it builds up to the entire reality field. Memes propagate in the thus constructed reality field by means of resonance.

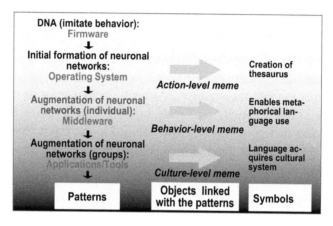

Figure 2.6. *The structure of meme*

Figure 2.7 illustrates how memes propagate in the reality field. The process of propagation is facilitated by symbolization. A symbolized meme enables people to think on abstract levels.

2.3.3. *Characteristics of meme propagation*

A meme is defined as a matrix-like construct that consists of multiple layers and a number of elements. The feeling of reality that an individual experiences is formed by integrating responses generated by the acceptor elements whose structure is defined similarly to that of the structured meme. However, the response sensitivity of the individual's acceptor elements is shaped by experience, and thus it exhibits individual differences depending on the individual's experience.

While a meme is propagating in the network of individuals, the differences in reality responses by individuals also propagate. This implies that the meme may be altered in the propagation process.

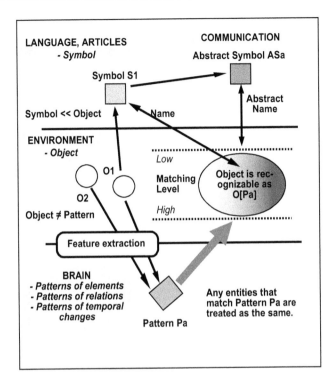

Figure 2.7. *Propagation of meme*

Figure 2.8 depicts the cultural evolution of a meme. It also demonstrates that some amount of fluctuation could appear in the flow of meme quantity and quality because the propagation cannot completely reflect the complexity of the environment.

2.4. NDHB-model/RT[2]

On the basis of O-SCFT, we have developed NDHB-model/RT as an architecture model that consists of a behavioral processing system and a memory processing system that interact with each other as autonomous systems. The interactions are cyclic, and memory develops and evolves as time goes by. NDHB-model/RT represents *consciousness* as one-dimensional

---

2 The description of this section is from section *C* of our article [KIT 15b].

linear operations, i.e. language, corresponding to System 2 of Two Minds, and *unconsciousness* including emotion as a hydrodynamic flow of information in multidimensional parallel operations in the neural networks, corresponding to System 1 of Two Minds. NDHB-model/RT has autonomous memory systems that mediate between consciousness and unconsciousness to display the dynamic interactions between them.

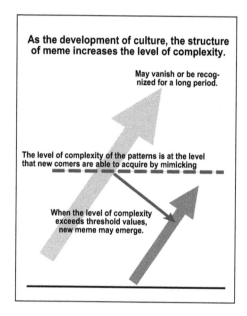

Figure 2.8. *Evolution of meme*

NDHB-model/RT suggests that the brain consists of the following three nonlinearly connected layers. Behavioral decisions and action selections are made by integrating the results of operations of these three layers (repeated from section 2.2.3):

– *C layer*: conscious state layer, i.e. System 2 of Two Minds;

– *A^2BC layer*: autonomous-automatic behavior control layer, i.e. System 1 of Two Minds;

– *B layer*: bodily state layer.

The B layer prioritizes the 17 behavioral goals, i.e. happiness types defined by Morris [MOR 06], such as "target happiness for an achiever", "cooperative happiness for a helper", "rhythmic happiness for a dancer", and so on. The other two layers interact with each other in order to derive the next behavior that should satisfy the highest prioritized goal. In normal situations in our daily life, temporal changes in the environment impose the strongest constraint on the decision of the next behavior, and thus the A^2BC layer plays a more dominant role than the C layer in organizing behavior. To put it simply, in our daily life we act more by reflex than by reasoning.

The next behavior is determined by extracting objects from the ever-changing environment and attaching values to them according to the degree of the strength of the resonance with what is stored in the autonomic memory system. This is followed by deliberate judgment by using the knowledge associated with the highly valued objects. The former is controlled by the processes in the A^2BC layer, System 1; the latter, by the processes in the C layer, System 2.

2.5. MHP/RT: Model human processor with real-time constraints[3]

NDHB-model/RT can be simulated by the architecture model, model human processor with real-time constraints (MHP/RT) [KIT 12a, KIT 11a, KIT 13]. MHP/RT focuses on synchronization between System 1 and System 2 in the information flow under O-PDP. More specifically, MHP/RT deals with one aspect of working of NDHB model/RT, which is synchronization between conscious system and unconscious system in the ever-changing environment where human beings make decisions and action selections to behave properly.

Figure 2.9 depicts the outline of MHP/RT. It is a *real* brain model composed of unconscious processes of System 1 and conscious processes of System 2 at the same level. There are two distinctive information flows: System 1 and System 2 receive input from the perceptual information processing system in one way, and from the memory processing system in another way. System 1 and System 2 work autonomously and synchronously without any superordinate–subordinate hierarchical relationships but interact

---

3 The description of this section is from section *D* of our article [KIT 15b].

with each other when necessary. In Figure 2.9, solid lines and dotted lines indicate the path associated with System 1 and the System 2, respectively. These two flows are synchronized before carrying out some behavior.

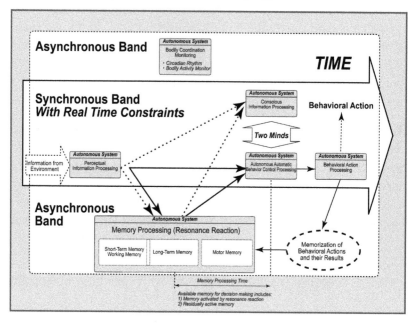

Figure 2.9. *Outline of MHP/RT (adapted from our article [KIT 15b], Figure 2). Solid lines indicates information for System 1 based processing and dotted lines indicates information for System 2 based processing. These two flows are synchronized before carrying out some behavior*

2.5.1. *MHP/RT's basic flow*[4]

As depicted in Figure 2.9, MHP/RT operates in two bands, the asynchronous band and the synchronous band. The bodily coordination monitoring system and the memory processing system operate in the asynchronous band. The perceptual information processing system, conscious information processing system, autonomous automatic behavior control processing system and behavioral action processing aystem operate in the

---

4 The description of this section is from section 3.1.1 of our article [KIT 13].

synchronous band. These systems work autonomously. System 1 of the Two Minds corresponds to the autonomous automatic behavior control processing system, and System 2 corresponds to the conscious information processing system.

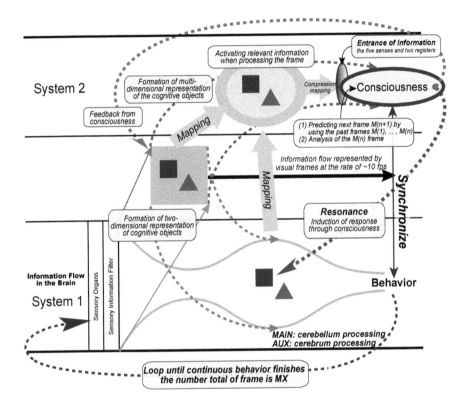

Figure 2.10. *MHP/RT (adapted from our article [KIT 12a])*

MHP/RT works as follows (Figure 2.10):

1) inputting information from the environment and the individual;

2) building a cognitive frame in working memory, which resides between the conscious process, System 2, and the unconscious process, System 1, to interface them – depicted between System 1 and System 2;

3) resonating the cognitive frame with autonomous long-term memory to make the relevant information stored in long-term memory available; cognitive frames are updated at a certain rate and the contents in the cognitive frames are continuously input to long-term memory to make pieces of information in long-term memory accessible to System 1 and System 2;

4) mapping the results of resonance on consciousness to form a reduced representation of the input information;

5) predicting future cognitive frames to coordinate input and working memory, corresponding to either decision-making or action selection depending on the time difference between the time when the prediction is made and the time when an event associated with the prediction takes palce, namely, whether the prediction is made mainly by System 2, decision-making, or by System 1, action selection.

The density of information in working memory is the product of the updating rate of the cognitive frame and the degree of fineness of the information represented in the cognitive frame. When the system is under the control of automatic behavior, i.e. under control of System 1, the updating rate of the cognitive frame tends to be high; however, the degree of fineness of the information represented in the cognitive frame is coarse. When the system is under the control of consciousness, i.e. under control of System 2, the updating rate of the cognitive frame and the degree of fineness of the information are flexibly determined by the context.

2.5.2. *Basic MHP/RT behaviors*

At a given time (T), MHP/RT's state is viewed by the following two ways:

1) which part of MHP/RT is working;

2) which content MHP/RT is processing.

In the following sections, the "which part" question will be discussed in section 2.5.2.1, and the "for what" question will be discussed in section 2.5.2.2.

2.5.2.1. *Four operation modes of MHP/RT*[5]

At a given time (), MHP/RT's state is considered from the viewpoint "which part of MHP/RT is working". In MHP/RT as illustrated by Figure 2.10, behavior is the outcome of activities in System 1 and System 2 both of which use working memory to prepare for the next action. Depending on the situation, behavior is driven mainly by either System 1 or System 2. Both systems work *synchronously* by sharing working memory. The former is called Mode 1, and the latter is called Mode 2. However, in some situations, both work *asynchronously*, Mode 3, or independently, Mode 4; working memory may be shared weakly or used solely for one of these layers (see Table 2.3):

– *Mode 1 (System 1 controls behavior)*: when System 1 governs behavior, the updating rate of the cognitive frame is the fastest and the system behaves unconsciously. The system refers to the memory that is activated via the resonance reaction, and the outcome of behavior is consciously monitored, which is mission of System 2 in this mode. As long as the output of behavior is consistent with the representation of the contents of activated memory, or prediction, no feedback control is applied. No serious decision-making is required but a series of unconscious action selections would result in smooth behavior. An example of this behavior mode is riding a bicycle on a familiar road.

– *Mode 3 (System 1 and System 2 are weakly coupled)*: in some cases, it is not necessary to monitor the behavior with high frequency. As a result, System 2 may initiate tasks that are not directly relevant to unconscious behavior. In such a situation, consciousness is free from behavior that is tightly embedded in the environment. For example, while waiting for his/her name to be called in a lobby of a hospital, he/she may read a book. In this case, at the time when his/her name is called, he/she would be able to stand up immediately to start walking to the consultation room. In his/her working memory, the pointer to the action would be kept active while reading a book and waiting for the announcement. This mode is characterized by weak coupling of System 1 and System 2, which means that pieces of information that reside in working memory are shared by System 1 and System 2, and therefore they could trigger the processes carried out by System 1 and System 2. And then, Mode 1 or Mode 2 takes over the operation. The shared information originates from perceptual encodings of the environment.

---

5 The description of this section is from section 3.2.1 of our article [KIT 13].

– *Mode 4 (System 1 and System 2 are isolated)*: in other cases, System 2 would initiate an independent process than System 1 is currently engaging. For example, he/she may use a mobile phone to talk with a friend while riding a bicycle, in which he/she might think deliberately to provide topics to enjoy conversation. In this case, his working memory would be used for two independent processes: talking with the friend over phone and riding bicycle safely. When encountering a dangerous situation, the system needs to take care of it primarily, which means that he/she needs to quit the phone conversation and use his/her working memory for controlling bicycle. Switching the part of memory used for the phone call to the bicycle ride would cause a certain amount of delay in action. This mode is characterized by isolation of System 1 from System 2, which means that each uses different portion of working memory for the respective processes. System 2 could be either totally detached from System 1, e.g. daydreaming, or in the deliberate thinking mode like Mode 2, in which System 2 mainly controls behavior and System 1 works under the control of System 2 by using the area of working memory for this process. Mode 3 and Mode 4 are similar because the process System 1 takes control and the Mode 3 and Mode 4 initiated by System 2 are carried out quasi-independently, but they are different in terms of the usage of working memory, i.e. Mode 3 has the area in working memory that holds information available to the two processes but Mode 4 does not.

– *Mode 2 (System 2 controls behavior)*: when System 2 governs behavior, the systems try to behave according to the image System 2 created or meditate with no bodily movement. The least resources are allocated for initiating behavior according to input from the environment. This corresponds to a situation in which the amount of flow of information in System 1 is small. Working memory is occupied by activities related to System 2. However, the sensory-information filter functions so that the system can react to a sudden interruption from the environment (e.g. a phone call).

Mode 1, or System 1 control mode, would require least cognitive resources for stringing pieces of behavior in the ever-changing environment. On the other hand, Mode 2, or System 2 control mode, would consist of resource consuming activities including reasoning, recalling weak memory, etc. System 1 control may break down due to unexpected changes in the environment, which would be detected by monitoring activity of System 2, leading to System 2 control mode for searching for procedures for escaping from the undesirable situation. Note that, in daily life, human beings are normally in System 1 control mode because human beings normally prefer effortless behavior, but are occasionally forced to operate in System 2 control mode for the purpose of resuming "normal" System 1 control mode easily and as soon as possible.

Synchronous Mode	
Mode 1: System 1 controls behavior	Skilled performance, i.e. no serious decision-making is necessary for most of behavior but still necessary to decide whether to continue, change, or terminate actions, but most of behavior can be regarded as a series of effortless action selections.
Mode 2: System 2 controls behavior	Unskilled activities, e.g. learning, thinking, etc.; a series of serious decision-makings will be required.
Asynchronous Mode	
Mode 3: System 1 and System 2 are weakly coupled	Concentrating on skilled activities; Shared use of working memory; Easy to resume to Mode 1 or 2 when necessary
Mode 4: System 1 and System 2 are isolated	Unconcentrated activities; Separate use of working memory; Time lag in resuming to Mode 1 or 2 activities when necessary

Table 2.3. *Four operation modes of MHP/RT and their relationships to decision-making and action selection*

2.5.2.2. *Four processing modes of MHP/RT*[6]

MHP/RT assumes that at a particular time *before the event*, say T_{before}, we engage in conscious processes of System 2 and unconscious processes System 1 concerning the event. At a particular time *after the event*, we engage in conscious processes and unconscious processes. What we can do before and after the event is strongly constrained by the Newell's time scale of human action as shown by Figure 2.11. It indicates that System 2 carries out the processes surrounded by a round-cornered rectangle with dotted lines, whereas System 1 does those surrounded by a round-cornered rectangle with solid lines.

---

6 The description of this section is basically from section 3.2.3 of our article [KIT 13].

MHP/RT works under the following four processing modes, ordered from the past to the future:

– *System 2 before mode*: conscious use of long-term memory before the event, i.e. System 2's operation for anticipating the future event or decision-making;

– *System 1 before mode*: unconscious use of long-term memory before the event, i.e. System 1's operation for automatic preparation for the future event or action selection;

– *System 1 after mode*: unconscious use of long-term memory after the event, i.e. System 1's operation for automatic tuning of long-term memory related with the past event;

– *System 2 after mode*: conscious use of long-term memory after the event, i.e. System 2's operation for reflecting on the past event.

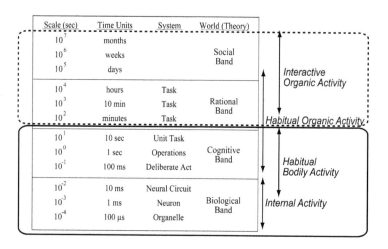

Figure 2.11. *Newell's time scale of human action [NEW 90] and behavioral characteristics of each band*

Figure 2.12 illustrates the four processing modes along the time dimension expanding before and after the event, which is shown as a *boundary event*. Table 2.4 shows the resulting four processing modes of *in situ* human behavior; at each moment, along the time dimension one behaves in one of the four processing modes and he/she switches among them depending on the internal and external states.

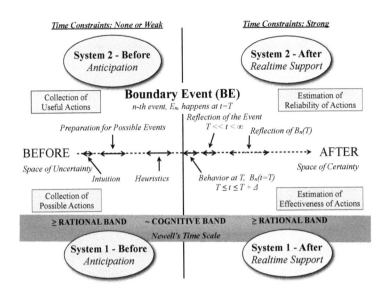

Figure 2.12. *How the four processing modes work (adapted from our article [KIT 13])*

2.5.2.3. *Four processing modes and adaptation*[7]

For MHP/RT, an event corresponds to a branch point where it can select an action from the alternatives under a specific environmental condition. The environment makes chaotic changes, and human beings, modeled by MHP/RT, are required to develop an adaptive system that is capable of dealing with a set of events that take place in such an environment. An event may result in selection of an action that is associated with one of four possible action categories, as defined by four processing modes. An event could be a future event or a past event, and it could be processed consciously or unconsciously. These are the four possibilities when we think about an event along the time dimension. An action selection will affect the future course of action selections, and the execution of the selected actions will change environmental conditions. The mode selection is carried out empirically. Under the condition of strong time constraints and the chaotic environment, the results of execution of selected actions would become unreliable, and it is required to repair the undesirable situations. In this situation, flexibility is required in selecting appropriate actions in response to the unpredictable

---

7 The description of this section is basically from section 3.2.3. of our article [KIT 13].

changes in the environment. The mechanism of switching among the four processing modes relative to a series of events makes possible the high-level empirical adaptation to the ever-changing environment.

	System 2 Conscious Processes		System 1 Unconscious Processes	
	Before	After	Before	After
Time Constraints	none or weak	exist	none or weak	exist
Network Structure	feedback	feedback	feed-forward + feedback	feed-forward + feedback
Processing	main serial conscious process + subsidiary parallel process	main serial conscious process + subsidiary parallel process	simple parallel process	simple parallel process
Newell's Time Scale	Rational/ Social	Rational/ Social	Biological/ Cognitive	Biological/ Cognitive

Table 2.4. *Four Processing Modes [KIT 11a]*

2.6. Two Minds and emotions [8]

As described in the previous sections, human behavior can be viewed as the integration of output of Systems 1, i.e. unconscious automatic processes, and System 2, i.e. conscious deliberate processes. System 1 activates a sequence of automatic actions in System 1 before mode. System 2 monitors the performance of System 1 according to the plan it has created, and it activates future possible courses of actions as well in System 2 before mode. At the same time, when these forward processes are working, System 1 and System 2 deal with the outcome of the forward processes by estimating the results of the performance of System 1 in System 1 after mode and the performance of System 2 in System 2 after mode. The result of estimation could be either good or bad in terms of the active goal at the moment controlled by MSA discussed in section 2.1, and it would generate *emotions* depending on the degree of goodness or badness of the estimation in the context of the current goal. Emotions are generated through the dynamics of the parallel processing of System 1 and System 2, which is called O-PDP

---

8 The description of this section is basically from section III of our article [KIT 15b].

discussed in section 1.2.1. This section discusses how emotion generation process is integrated with MHP/RT.

2.6.1. Dynamics of consciousness–emotion interaction: an explanation by MHP/RT

2.6.1.1. Interaction between consciousness and emotion

The processes in the A^2BC layer and those in the C layer are not independent. Rather, they interact with each other very intensely in some cases but very weakly in other cases. We investigate this issue in more detail below.

2.6.1.1.1. Onset of consciousness

With the onset of arousal, the sensory organs begin to collect environmental information. This information flows into the brain, and the volume of information flow grows rapidly. As the information flow circulates in the neural networks, the center of the flow gradually emerges. It corresponds to the location where the successive firings of the neural networks concentrate. At this time, the center of information flow induces activities in the C layer via the cross-links in the neural networks.

2.6.1.1.2. Conscious activities

Figure 2.13 depicts the state of the brain when consciousness starts working. The location of consciousness is indicated as a dot in the C layer. In many cases, the working of consciousness includes such cognitive activities as comprehension of self-orientation and the individual's circumstances. The judgment on what decision-making is needed for the current situation is equivalent to initiating some action to move the location of consciousness to an appropriate direction. The direction of movement is determined by the information needs at that time. It could move either in the direction in which the initial information will be deepened (left in the figure) or to the direction in which the initial information will be widened (right in the figure). The density of information would change depending on how far the center of consciousness would have moved. However, the location of the consciousness would not move when carrying out a routine task.

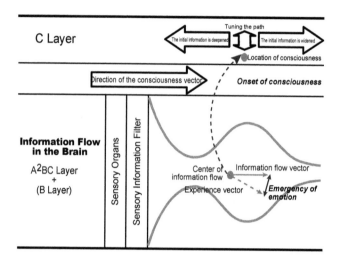

Figure 2.13. *Onset of consciousness and emergence of emotion (adapted from our article [KIT 15b])*

2.6.1.1.3. Emergence of emotion

After the onset of consciousness, a new thread of information coming into the brain via the sensory organs triggers successive firing within the neural networks. This causes a new information flow in the brain that reflects the past experience that resonates with the input information. If there is a discrepancy between the new information flow (the dotted line in the figure) and the existing information flow (the solid line in the figure), emotion emerges. Emotion works to reduce the amount of discrepancy.

2.6.1.1.4. Determination of next behavior

When the A^2BC layer works continuously within its capacity, consciousness does not interfere with the working of the A^2BC layer but monitors the individual's behavior, prepares for the next behavior, and/or ponders issues that come to mind. However, if the A^2BC layer has difficulty in determining the next behavior, the C layer takes over and determines it. However, note that decision-making deals with planning for future behavior in the "System 2 before mode". Actions that will be taken actually in the ever-changing real world are determined by the system flexibly in an ad-lib fashion in the "System 1 before mode".

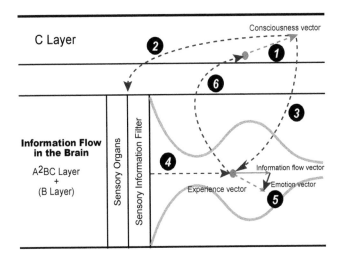

Figure 2.14. *Determination of next behavior
(adapted from our article [KIT 15b])*

2.6.1.1.5. Summary

The following points depict the flow of the processes that takes place (see Figure 2.14):

1) consciousness determines the next behavior by considering the current state of emotion and the self-recognition;

2) consciousness tunes the orientation of the sensory organs in preparation for initiating the next behavior just determined;

3) consciousness commands initiating the next behavior;

4) the behavior results in changes in the information flow;

5) the direction of emotion changes;

6) the new state of emotion affects the process of determining the next behavior.

2.6.1.2. *Synchronization between the C layer and the A^2BC layer: MHP/RT's perspective*

We assume that the C layer and the A^2BC layer operate together in order to determine the next behavior. However, as described above, the interaction between them could be weak or strong, depending on the situation. There thus needs to be a synchronization mechanism for them to work together appropriately. The most important assumption of the MHP/RT is that the human brain works under real-time constraints governed by the environment, largely uncontrollable from the brain. Therefore, detection of discrepancy is closely related with the mechanism of synchronization between consciousness and unconsciousness. The degree of discrepancy could be measured by the amount of efforts to reestablish good synchronization between the two systems.

We suggest that the visual frame reconstruction process in the C layer should be used for establishing synchronization between the C layer and the A^2BC layer. In Figure 2.9, this synchronization process is indicated schematically as an arrow with the label "Two Minds". The C layer predicts the representation of the visual frame that should appear in the future and uses it for synchronization. The information flow for this process is indicated in the dotted lines in Figure 2.9, which occurs in the characteristic times surrounded by a round-cornered rectangle with dotted lines as shown in Figure 2.11. On the other hand, when the A^2BC layer mainly controls the behavior, the visual frame rate would be around 10 frames per second. The information flows as indicated by the solid lines in Figure 2.9, with the characteristic times in the a round-cornered rectangle with solid lines, as shown in Figure 2.11.

When the C layer controls the behavior as in the former case, the rate would become lower and vary depending on the interest of consciousness. In the latter case, the C layer would monitor the self-behavior by occasionally matching the expected visual frame and the real visual frame in the A^2BC layer. For the former situation, the visual frame density is high but the information density is low; for the latter situation, the visual frame density is low but the information density is high. Discrepancy would be detected easier in the former case than the latter.

2.6.2. *Taxonomy of emotions: behavioral perspective*

Table 2.5 summarizes the relationships between Two Minds and emotions as a combination of the states of the C layer and A^2BC layer. The top half of the table lists the kinds of decision-making that the C layer would do before some event takes place. Depending on the intensity of the signals emitted from the A^2BC layer and the self-estimate of the state of the system, the C layer decides to do something with large effort, small effort, or just do nothing, or do nothing intentionally. Note that no emotion will take place at the time when the C layer makes decisions concerning the system's future.

Case	System 2's before-event expectation				
	C layer's before-event decision-making	Signasl emitted from A^2BC layer	C layer's estimate when expectation was formed		
1	do something with small effort	stable (no signal)	relaxed		
2	do nothing intentionally	bad	prepared for bad		
3	do something with large effort	bad	positive		
4	do something with large effort	good	strongly positive		
5	do nothing	good	calm		
Case	System 2's after-event decision-making				
	C layer after-event decision-making	Signals emitted from A^2BC layer	C layer's estimate when decision-making was done	Result of A^2BC layer's action	Emotion after A^2BC layer's action was taken
6	do something with small effort	good	good	+	satisfaction
				−	shock, lostness
7	do nothing intentionally	bad	bad	+	amazement, pleasure
				−	regret, despair
8	do something with large effort	bad	uneasy	+	self-praise
				−	apology
9	do nothing	good	fearful	+	relief
				−	regret

Table 2.5. *Relationships between Two Minds and emotions (adapted from our article [KIT 15b])*

On the other hand, as shown in the bottom half of the table, emotions will emerge when actions are carried out by the A^2BC layer. A specific emotion type would emerge depending on the combinations of the possible states of the following four conditions:

1) the signal intensity of the A^2BC layer;

2) C-layer's estimate of the system state;

3) the nature of C layer's decision-making;

4) the result of A^2BC layer's action.

For example, in Case 9, though the A^2BC layer emits good signals, the C layer estimates the situation to be fearful. It decides not to do anything. However, the A^2BC layer reacts to the situation autonomously and the situation eventually turns good. The C layer feels relieved. In summary, this table provides a taxonomy of emotions in terms of the activities of theA^2BC layer and C layer.

3

Layered-structure of Memory
and its Development

The human memory system is an integration of three distributed memory systems associated with respective autonomous organic systems; the perceptual system that takes care of sensory input from the environment, the conscious system that performs deliberate decision-making and the unconscious system that carries out action selections in the environment. It works as a memory component in the comprehensive brain model, MHP/RT [KIT 13], which is capable of simulating daily human behavior considering the real-time constraints that should define strong mutual dependencies among the three systems. This chapter reconsiders MHP/RT's memory system by mapping it on the real interconnections between the cranial nerves and the spinal nerves to obtain a topological representation of the distributed memory system.

3.1. MHP/RT modules and their associated memories

The human memory system is constructed as the result of a continuous cyclic loop of perception and movement as shown by Figure 3.1. This process chart essentially shows that memory is created via working of autonomous nervous systems that operate along the information flow from the *sensory nervous system* to *somatic nervous system* via *interneurons* under the time constraints that should reflect the environmental conditions at the time of each operation. Operations are the results of a sequence of selecting an action followed by its execution. Our MHP/RT describes how it is carried out through coordination of the autonomous systems that comprise "synchronous band" as shown in Figure 2.9, i.e. perceptual information processing, conscious information processing, autonomous automatic behavior control processing and behavioral action processing autonomous systems. The human memory system is considered as an integration of three distributed memory systems associated with respective autonomous organic systems; the perceptual system that takes care of sensory input from the environment, the conscious system that performs deliberate decision making and the unconscious system that carries out action selections in the environment.

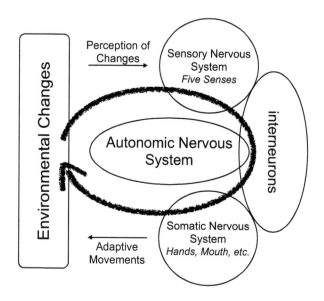

Figure 3.1. *Continuous cyclic loop of perception and movement (repeated from Introduction)*

Structural features of a memory system can be derived by considering the fact that each autonomous system in synchronous band of MHP/RT has its own memory; each memory system records the traces of its working over time. Therefore, the human memory structure is modeled conceptually as shown in Figure 3.2. MHP/RT assumes that memory is organized by multidimensional memory frame (MD memory frame) for storing information. As the main modules in the synchronous band, MHP/RT consists of perceptual system, conscious processing system and unconscious (autonomous automatic behavior control) processing system. Figure 3.2 illustrates memory systems associated with these main modules. In addition, those memories are added that are created by integrating individual memories associated with System 1 and System 2, respectively, and that is created by analyzing phoneme structures associated with language activities.

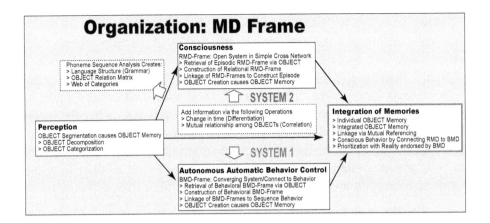

Figure 3.2. *Multidimensional memory frame (adapted from our article [KIT 13])*

3.1.1. *Memory formation process*

MHP/RT starts action selection processes by *object cognition*. It occurs as follows [KIT 13]: collecting information from the environment via perceptual sensors; integrating and segmenting the collected information, centering on visually collected objects; and continuing these processes until the necessary objects to live in the environment are obtained. These objects are then used independently in Systems 1 and 2 of Two Minds, and memorized after integrating related entities associated with each system.

Due to the limitation of the brain's processing capability, the range of integration is limited; therefore, System 1 memory and System 2 memory should differ. However, they could share objects originating from perceptual sensors. The types of information to be memorized are not the four-dimensional values of objects but a set of differential features of objects associated with strong variations, phase change points, or boundaries, and mutual relationships among them. Such quantities as time and distance, direct derivatives of the four-dimensional values of the objects, are reconstructed from the memory when the memory of the objects are needed in such a way that they are consistent with the environmental conditions at that time. *What* people would do in a specific situation is dictated by the contents stored in the MD memory frames and *how* people would do is determined by the behavior generation processes of MHP/RT.

When objects, that are the result of the just-finished integration and segmentation process, are processed in the next cycle, representation of the objects may serve as the common elements to combine System 1 memory and System 2 memory to form an intersystem memory. We call this memory the MD memory frames. They should result in a distributed layered memory structure because of the multiplicity of MD perceptions and MD motor activities. And then activations in the memory network always descend from perceptual memory to the rest of the memory structure. Multidimensionality in both perceptual and motor processing works as a kind of filter to prune ineffective connections.

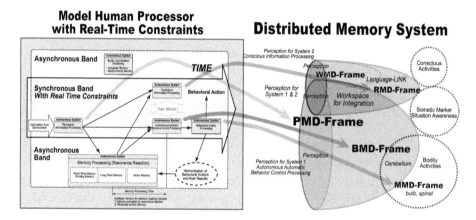

Figure 3.3. *Relationships between the autonomous processing modules in MHP/RT and multidimensional memory frames in the distributed memory system (adapted from our article [KIT 14c])*

3.1.2. *MD memory frames*

Figure 3.3 illustrates how each MD memory frames are created as the result of working of autonomous processes in MHP/RT and how MD memory frames are mutually interrelated. This essentially details the process "memorization of behavioral actions and their results" (shown by the dotted oval in Figure 3.3) of MHP/RT as shown in Figure 2.9, by considering neuronal activities that actually take place. The basic idea is that each autonomous system has its own memory. Figure 3.4 shows a close-up view of the distributed memory system. There are five kinds of MD memory frames.

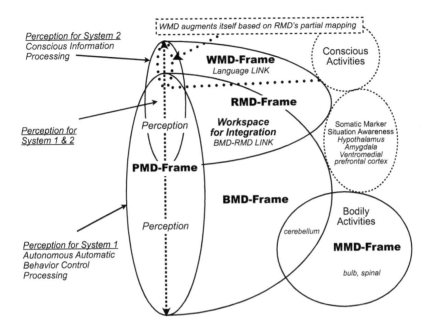

Figure 3.4. *A close-up view of the distributed memory system*

– *Perceptual multidimensional (PMD) memory frame*:   constitutes perceptual memory as a relational matrix structure. It collects information from external objects followed by separating it into a variety of perceptual information, and recollects the same information in the other situations, accumulating the information from the objects via a variety of different processes. PMD memory frame incrementally grows as it creates memory from the input information and matches it against the past memory in parallel.

– *Motion multidimensional (MMD) memory frame*: constitutes behavioral memory as a matrix structure. The behavioral action processing starts when unconscious autonomous behavior shows after one's birth. It gathers a variety of perceptual information as well to connect muscles with nerves using spinals as a reflection point. In accordance with one's physical growth, it widens the range of activities the behavioral action processing can cover autonomously.

– *Behavior multidimensional (BMD) memory frame*: is the memory structure associated with the autonomous automatic behavior control processing. It combines a set of MMD memory frames into a manipulable unit.

– *Relation multidimensional (RMD) memory frame*: is the memory structure associated with the conscious information processing. It combines a set of BMD memory frames into a manipulable unit. The role BMD memory frames play for RMD memory frame is equivalent to the role MMD memory frames play for BMD memory frame.

– *Word multidimensional (WMD) memory frame*: is the memory structure for language. It is constructed on a very simple one-dimensional array.

The entire memory system is topologically shown in Figures 3.4 and 3.5. Figure 3.4 shows respective memory systems that interact with each other, and Figure 3.5 shows their relationships along the time dimension. Figure 3.5 shows the relationships among the five MD memory frames in terms of how they are organized in a layered structure, how a flux of information flows through the MD memory frames from the top layer to the bottom layer and how the MD memory frames evolve through a cyclic network structure in a bottom-up way.

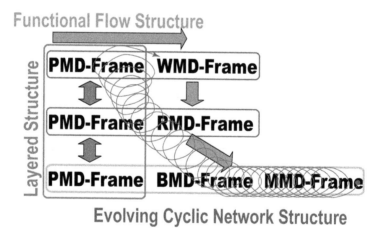

Figure 3.5. *Functional flow structure, layered structure and evolving cyclic network structure (adapted from our article [KIT 14c])*

From the viewpoint of layered structure, Figure 3.5 is explained as follows: the bottom layer creates a behavioral econetwork for the individual. This is a cyclic network starting from PMD toward MMD, and returning to PMD. The middle layer resides on the behavioral econetwork for the individual. In this layer, we acquire the meaning of behavior in the social ecology. The top layer is controlled by words. It consists of simple one-dimensional array of symbols, logically constructed language, grammars that specify language use, etc. This layered structure is used when reading information from memory, which determines actually read memory under the influence of reward (somatic marker) and status of short-term memory. The somatic nervous system that leads to BMD is created autonomously under the constraints defined by the mutual relationships between nerves, muscles and skeletons. This determines what is written in the memory. Note that somatic markers that associate respective memory with rewards have strong effect on the behavior of memory system.

3.1.3. *Memory functions via resonance*

At a given moment, MHP/RT is working in one of the four operation modes (see section 2.5.2.1). However, the memory system works autonomously to make part of long-term memory active so that it can be used in System 1 and/or System 2 processing through resonance processes. However, as depicted in Figure 3.6, how the memory system reacts to the environment may depend on the degree of time constraints that the human–environment system imposes on itself. When real-time constraints are strong, slow memory processes that use long-term memory do not participate in the processing. In other words, only the unconscious side of the Two Minds system, System 1, works and has a chance to use memory through resonance. In contrast, with few real-time constraints, the conscious and unconscious systems work collaboratively in some cases and independently in other cases. Both systems have a chance to use as many resonated contents as possible.

3.1.4. *Memory operates in pipelining*

At a given moment, MHP/RT is processing one of four content types: a future event consciously or unconsciously, or a past event consciously or unconsciously. For future/conscious processing, MHP/RT uses memory that conveys a sequence of actions with symbolic representations for accomplishing a currently held goal. For future/unconscious processing, it uses memory that is associated with an automatic sequence of actions that should lead to the goal. For past/conscious processing, it reflects on and elaborates a certain symbolic event by using activated pieces of knowledge through resonance processes. For past/unconscious processing, existing memory is modified by using activated non-symbolic pieces of knowledge that is currently activated in working memory.

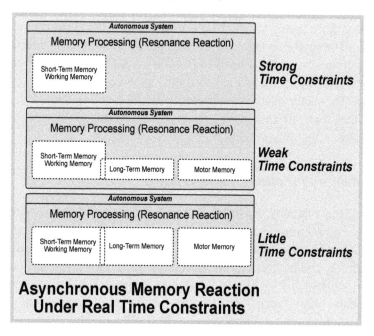

Figure 3.6. *Memory reaction under real-time constraints (adapted from [KIT 12b])*

It is important to note that memory activation is a totally parallel process; therefore, there is no way of knowing which part of activated memory is used. It depends completely on which object MHP/RT is processing. MHP/RT's resonance process makes available the relevant part of activated knowledge through resonance. Along the time dimension, MHP/RT, working in one of four operation modes, switches among the four processing modes and uses activated knowledge through resonance. MHP/RT's processing is a pipeline process of four primitive processes. The nature of this pipelining may change depending on the nature of the task. When learning a new task, it is impossible to foresee the future; therefore, past/conscious processing may dominate. In contrast, for example, when an experienced piano player is playing a well-practiced tune, future/unconscious processing may dominate.

3.2. Hierarchical structure of human action selection

With the cyclic processes of action selection and memorization as shown in Figures 3.1 and 3.3, we develop his/her memory and show distinct behavioral characteristics as we grow. In other words, one develops *individual* MD memory frames as one interacts with the environment and select actions by running MHP/RT. This section suggests that the cyclic processes results in a hierarchical structure of action selection and summarizes what it means according to several age ranges [KIT 14a].

3.2.1. *Three-layered structure of interneurons system*

Interneurons intervene the sensory nervous system that is responsible for processing sensory information and the somatic nervous system that is associated with the voluntary control of body movements via skeletal muscles to form complex paired structures of perception and motion. It consists of direct feed-forward connections from perception to motion, and more complex connections with feedback loops using the interneurons to form three distinguishable layers. Table 3.1 summarizes the points.

There are two layers in the autonomous automatic behavior control processing, both of which are controlled by feed-forward loop:

– *Layer 1:* the first layer is associated with reactive activities carried out by the spinal nerves characterized by automatic and simple reflexive movements;

– *Layer 2:* the second layer is associated with reactive activities carried out by the bulb or the cerebellum characterized by automatic complex reflexive movements.

One layer is associated with the conscious information processing, controlled by feedback loops and the back propagation mechanism.

– *Layer 3:* the third layer is associated with activities carried out by the frontal lobe and the cerebrum characterized by deliberate movements.

3.2.2. *Formation process*

The following explains the developmental paths of the neural networks as human beings grow as the function of their ages.

Hierarchical Structure of Neural Networks	Hierarchical Structure of Cognitive Mechanism		
	System 1 of Two Minds		System 2
	Layer-1	Layer-2	Layer-3
	Multi-dimensional perception	Vision-oriented structural multi-dimensional perception	Language, one-dimensional sequence of sound, and nonverbal symbols
Architecture for Processing	autonomous automatic behavior control	autonomous automatic behavior control + conscious information processing when needed	Conscious information processing; natural formation of grammar; perceptron
Formation Process	genetic	genetic + epigenetic	epigenetic (meme)
Number Sense	multi-valued stimuli	voluntarily formed perceptron using visual patterns; comparative cognition	mathematics; deliberate consideration
Contents	any changes around the self	three-dimensional space recognition, linear continuous change, visual + auditory information	representation of procedural knowledge; continuity under non-linear links; structural decomposition and reconstruction; grammar and notation
Acquisition	experience	imitation of bodily movement	learning of formality + confirmation of the results of experience and procedural understanding; not systematic understanding; uncertain in reproduction
Role of Cognition	for individual; intuitive understanding; used for adaptive reaction	for individual and society; behavior-ecological understanding; used for habitual behavior	for society; conceptual understanding; used for sense making

Table 3.1. *Relationships between the hierarchical structure of cognitive mechanism and that of neural networks (adapted from our article [KIT 14a])*

– *Early stage: 0–6 years of age*: between 0–6 years of age, feed-forward loops are the dominant control mechanism and they establish fundamental relationships between the layers by means of "uplink". In the first half of this period, between 0–3 years of age, human beings establish interconnections between Layer 1 and Layer 2 as integrated movements of bodily actions on the basis of the relationships between the input from the perceptual system and the output expressed as reflexive movements, for example, simple utterances. In the latter half of this period, 4–6 years of age, human beings acquire the skill of behaving in relation with the other persons and the methods for conversing with others such as explanation formation via simple syntax.

– *Middle stage: 7–12 years of age*: later, between 7–12 years of age, human beings acquire the skill of logical thinking by means of the first order logic by using letters or symbols and that of cooperation with other people. These activities facilitate the development of interconnections among the three layers, resulting in very complex networks. The key is the existence of symbols that intervene various connections between input and output.

– *Later stage: 13–18 years of age*: then, between 13–18 years of age, feedback loops come into play, which are used to form language processing circuits in a single layer, Layer 3, by means of the learning mechanism such as the back propagation. Between 13–18 years of age, the interconnections of the neural networks evolve among the three layers. In this period, the ability of logical writing by using an ordinary language significantly affects the evolving process. Without language, structural recognition is formed dominantly via visual information. On the other hand, when accompanied with language, it makes it possible to represent the visual information in a highly logical way, the vision-based structural recognition is significantly augmented to become a structure that can be dealt with a language-based logic system.

– *Final stage: approximately 18 years of age*: finally, at approximately 18 years of age, feedback loops become dominant, which make it possible to form compound language-processing circuits by means of the learning mechanism such as the back propagation mechanism.

It is important to note that the "language" that each individual is doomed to use should affect the course of development of the individual. There are obvious differences in the syntax of languages among, for example, Japanese, English, French, and so on. Therefore, Japanese people, for example, tend to acquire the skill of visual perception to compensate for the weakness of their language. It is because their language is not good at representing logical relationships. Conscious processing of System 2 comes at the later stage of one's life. However, it poses strong constraints on the individual's developmental path, because it is language bound. This consideration sheds a new light on how the hierarchy of the neural networks should develop in the circumstances where we live.

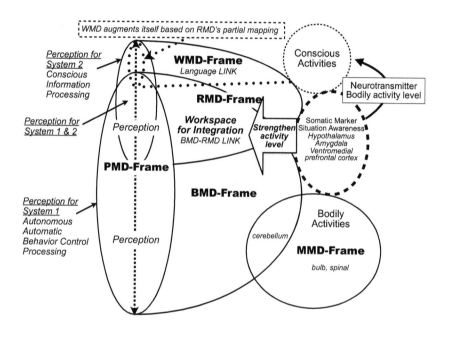

Figure 3.7. *MD-frames and emotion (an updated version of Figure 3.4)*

3.3. Emotion initiation via memory processes

As the last part of the description of memory, this section extends the explanation given in section 2.6 in terms of how emotion would be initiated via memory processes [KIT 15b]. Figure 3.7 illustrates processes in MD memory frames with the focus of emotion. Memory activation originates from perception and spreads in MD memory frames. In normal operation, active memory regions are used for organizing behavior. For the conscious system, most active memory regions would connect to consciousness and have effects on conscious activities. For the unconscious bodily movement system, the most active memory regions corresponding to respective body parts would directly guide action selections in parallel.

Somatic markers directly guide the action selections that are carried out in a feed-forward way. On the other hand, they have indirect effects on conscious activities by providing integrated information about the current status of the body via receptors of the conscious system where neurotransmitters' local density represents the integrated response to the current status of the body. In other words, emotion corresponds to the internal activities that coordinate conscious processes and unconscious processes to work coherently in the ever-changing environment.

As Damasio [DAM 99] puts it, emotion emerges when consciousness is recognized for the first time. Feeling appears when the emotion is analyzed ecologically and recognized at a later time.

4

Implication for Human–Machine Interaction: Autonomous System Interaction Design (ASID) based on NDHB-Model/RT

Traditional interactive systems transform input to the systems from the environment to output in the environment by using a set of rules. However, these systems are not intelligent enough to respond to an ever-changing environment including users. There are thus cases where inputs to a system may drift too far to be handled by the set of rules, and the system might respond inappropriately. This chapter discusses a new perspective on interactive system design. The key idea is to deal with interactive systems as autonomous systems that interact with users that are other autonomous systems, modeled by MHP/RT with MD memory frames, and designing interactive systems implies designing autonomous system interactions (ASIs) that establish natural cooperation among them.

4.1. Users modeled by MHP/RT with MD memory frames

In the previous chapters, we have described the entire model of users who interact with ever-changing environment and develop through the experience of moment-by-moment interactions. Figure 4.1 integrates the pieces to construct the entire complete model of human beings. It carries out the following processes in a cyclic way; perceive the external and internal environments, resonate memory by firing relevant portion of memory, synchronize fast and automatic unconscious process and slow and deliberate conscious process in four processing modes of MHP/RT and reconstruct memory reflecting on the results of action selection and decision-making. In addition, emotions interfere with the cyclic process when necessary to make the model revert to normal paths. The processing modules function autonomously and therefore coordination of mutual modules to adapt to the ever-changing environment is carried out in a self-regulatory fashion. Given the understanding of the users as modeled by this way, this chapter considers the relationships between users and interactive systems at a relatively abstract level to see the conditions for establishing good relationships between them.

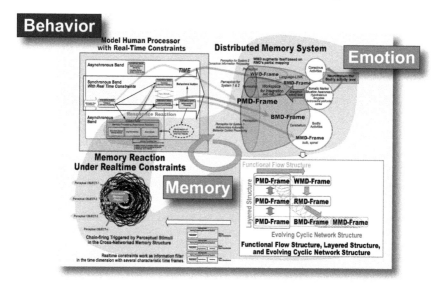

Figure 4.1. *Users modeled by MHP/RT with MD memory frames*

4.2. Autonomous systems versus linear systems

Human beings interact with an environment that includes interactive systems. The following sections start by describing a society of systems having the property of linearity or autonomy, followed by the needs that those systems must satisfy and the proposal of autonomous systems interaction that should meet the requirements.

4.2.1. *Linear systems*

Objects behaving in the environment are defined in four-dimensional space–time coordinates. A human being, as far as being viewed as a linear system, acquires information of behaving objects via its sensory organs as two-dimensional data. The four-dimensional data are reduced to two-dimensional data in this process. The input data are then used for representing their characteristics by means of static linear functions. When an objective of behavior is given, the linear system will behave by deriving static solutions by using the linear functions that best match the current situation.

Figure 4.2 illustrates a society of linear systems managing various situations by tuning the relationships among the constituent systems. However, there are situations where the current organization of the systems causes a large amount of stress in spite of efforts made to resolve the situations and they cannot behave properly. In these situations, the systems have to change themselves. However, the change may or may not produce good results. In the worst cases, the change may cause a rapid increase in stress and crash the system.

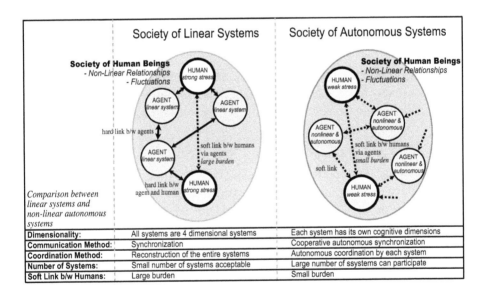

Comparison between linear systems and non-linear autonomous systems	Society of Linear Systems	Society of Autonomous Systems
Dimensionality:	All systems are 4 dimensional systems	Each system has its own cognitive dimensions
Communication Method:	Synchronization	Cooperative autonomous synchronization
Coordination Method:	Reconstruction of the entire systems	Autonomous coordination by each system
Number of Systems:	Small number of systems acceptable	Large number of ssystems can participate
Soft Link b/w Humans:	Large burden	Small burden

Figure 4.2. *Society of linear systems and society of autonomous systems*

4.2.2. *Autonomous systems*

Human beings viewed as autonomous systems represent behaving objects in the four-dimensional space–time environment via sensory organs. For example, the sense of taste is represented by six-dimensional data and the sense of sight is represented by four-dimensional data. The input data are processed mainly by the A^2BC layer and the B layer, and optionally by the C layer in the brain, and used to define functions that work in SMT and MSA with the real-time constraints defined by BIH. The functions accumulate personal four-dimensional experience continuously. When an objective of behavior is given, the autonomous system will behave by deriving effective regions so that the self will behave properly by using the functions.

When an autonomous system communicates with another one, it uses the effective region at each moment. This assures less stressful communication among autonomous systems than among linear systems (Figure 4.2).

4.3. Needs that a society of information systems must meet

We suggest that autonomy of systems is necessary for establishing an effective society of interactive systems because the current society has become rich and has to satisfy each individual's diverse needs. The needs of the society include the following:

– *Need for efficiency, effectivity and low price*:   This is satisfied by developing high-performance systems with integrated functionalities. However, it is important to match the performance of the systems with the performance of brain functioning by considering the characteristics of human beings based on NDHB model/RT.

– *Need for ease of use*: This depends on an individual's knowledge and its use. This need has priority over the need for efficiency, effectivity and low price. The use of knowledge is mainly defined by SMT.

– *Need for satisfaction*: This need depends on an individual's experience. This is satisfied by developing an autonomous systems society that can deal with diversity in the evaluation criteria and their temporal changes.

4.4. Outline of ASI

The current social system is built on the traditional interaction model that assumes linearity of the society. As described above, there are serious limitations in linear systems when trying to satisfy diverse individuals' needs. In the following, this chapter outlines autonomous systems interaction that should satisfy the above-mentioned needs for a society of information systems.

An autonomous system monitors its environment continuously and initiates communication with the other autonomous systems when needed. There are three purposes of ASI as follows:

– it helps enhance the autonomy of human beings;

– it adds autonomy to devices;

– it helps maintain harmony of the entire society.

In order to achieve these purposes, ASI includes the following characteristics:

– request for information;

– support for help;

– guide for action.

Initiation of communication includes such activities as (1) direct the other party's attention to the initiator and (2) synchronize activities among the participants. An autonomous system takes the initiative in order to maintain communication. There are two types of information in ASI. One is static information that is used for the analysis of objectives and evaluation. The other is dynamic information that is used for organizing future courses of behavior. The static information is acquired either by:

– monitoring without notice, which means that the system does not notice that it is monitored;

– monitoring with notice, in which the monitored system knows that it is being monitored.

The dynamic information is used for emergency control, supportive control, or full control.

In summary, consciousness and emotion function jointly for determining communication behavior. Figure 4.3 depicts an example of a society that is designed by means of ASI.

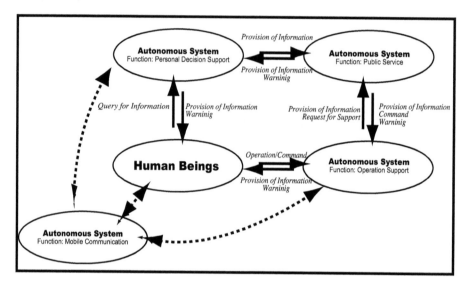

Figure 4.3. *An example of society composed of autonomous systems interaction (ASI)*

4.5. Conclusions

This chapter proposed a concept of ASI design that is most suitable for constructing a society of interactive systems including human beings. All the constituent systems are modeled and designed as autonomous systems, and thus interactions among them are symmetric. Coordination of systems in pursuit of satisfying the current objectives is achieved through participation of all the systems: each system behaves autonomously for achieving the objectives. Autonomous systems are designed by assuming that human beings behave according to the NDHB model/RT.

A society of systems that consists of personal decision support systems, operation support systems, mobile communication support systems and public support systems would be a typical organization of ASI as depicted in Figure 4.3. Each autonomous system has its characteristic regions in the spatial–temporal and information dimensions, and it decides what to do next by using a decision-making algorithm that is specific to the system. When deciding, the system monitors the other systems that are relevant to the current decision-making and requests information when necessary in order to make better decisions by considering the other systems' behavior. The systems iterate this fundamental coordination process to achieve a stable and effective solution for the current objectives.

PART 2

Theoretically Motivated Methodology for Understanding Users

5

Cognitive Chrono-ethnography

In the previous chapters, a cognitive architecture for action selection and memorization has been discussed. It provides the mechanism for analyzing how human beings would select their next actions in an ever-changing environment by synchronizing unconscious fast processes and conscious slow processes, and what would do by using MD memory frames, which themselves evolve over time as human beings interact with the environment by performing actions and reflecting on the results of performance. On the basis of this understanding of human beings' action selection and memorization, this chapter introduces a theoretically motivated study methodology for understanding human beings' activities in real life situations.

5.1. Understanding people's behavior in real life

A series of a person's action selections can be regarded as a result of moment-by-moment problem-solving activities. The *problem* in this situation is in realizing a goal state by successively applying moves in the problem space. Each move causes a transition from one state to another and the move finally chosen at a specific state depends on the available resources that he or she can manipulate during the allowed time. Remember that moves can happen in a varied timescale as indicated by Newell's time scale of human action (see Figure 2.11). If enough time is provided, it is possible for him or her to select a move that has a greater expected benefit. In this situation, he or she can utilize as much knowledge as possible to achieve better solutions. However, if not enough time is allowed, there is nothing for him or her but to choose an ordinary solution. In most situations, this is the one he or she has adopted most frequently in the similar situations to the current one in the past. This decision is done without deliberate consideration concerning possible future development of the course of actions. Using the terms introduced in section 2.5.2.2, the situations can be rephrased as follows: the former case is dominated by System 2 before mode, whereas the latter by System 1 before mode, respectively.

Understanding people's behavior in real life can be achieved by two-tiered research approach, that is *domain-independent theorization* and *domain-dependent instantiation*, or, theoretically motivated case studies. Domain-independent theorization deals with what people would do at abstract levels. This book suggests that NDHB-model/RT is *the* theory and MHP/RT provides a way for simulating human action selections on the basis of NDHB-model/RT.

This chapter and the following two chapters describe domain-dependent instantiation for understanding people's behavior in real life. This chapter explains a methodology cognitive chrono-ethnography (CCE) to be used in this research activity. CCE is derived by considering requirements that are imposed on a study methodology for dealing with people's action selections in time-critical real-world settings. It starts by describing the requirements for the methodology and providing the top level description of the CCE methodology.

The chapters to follow illustrate case studies to demonstrate what people actually do in real-world navigation. Navigation is an appropriate behavioral category to study with MHP/RT because: (1) both external and internal situations change as far as navigation continues, and synchronization of conscious processes with unconscious processes is definitely needed to produce coherent behavior in the ever-changing environment; (2) navigation can be either self-paced (internal control) or environment-paced (external control); and (3) navigation can be either fast or slow. Navigation can happen either in a real physical environment or in a virtual informational environment. No matter in which environment navigation takes place, action selections and memorization can be considered in the framework of NDHB model/RT and simulated by MHP/RT. This book takes two case studies concerning navigations with different characteristics. Chapter 6 concerns a relatively slow navigation, i.e. investigation of how elderly people use guide signs at train stations when they have to transfer lines, in addition to using facilities such as restrooms, lockers, elevators, telephones and so on. This situation is characterized by self-paced active information gathering to select next actions for accomplishing consciously managed explicit goals. Chapter 6 concerns a relatively fast navigation, i.e. investigation of valuable and useful information for drivers when driving unfamiliar roads. This situation is characterized by environment-paced passive information gathering to select next actions for accomplishing unconsciously managed implicit goals.

5.2. Cognitive chrono-ethnography

Our 24-hour day is roughly divided into three categories. The first is the hours for work to earn money, the second is the hours for biological activities to live and the third is the hours for the rest to spend time for feeling satisfaction or happiness, otherwise called leisure activities, such as playing sports, watching TV, driving a car, playing PC games, traveling, going to the movies, surfing the Web and so on. Not all but most activities categorized in the third category involve HMI and therefore its design should affect the performance of such activities. When it is well designed, the users have satisfactory experiences. Traditionally, the first two categories have been dealt with in such study fields as human factors and ergonomics. However, the third category has been little studied because of the diversity involved in such activities. This section starts by describing requirements for the methodology (CCE) to study people's behavior in real life that belongs to the third category and suggests four critical factors to be considered as the primary causes of the diversity, and must be disentangled by CCE to obtain coherent understanding of how daily behavior is organized.

5.2.1. *Requirements for the methodology (CCE) to study human beings' behavior in real life*

5.2.1.1. *What to understand*

Understanding human beings' daily action selections should come down to understanding relationships between memes that are active at the time the behavior was undertaken and the overtly observed behavior by taking into account those factors as Two Minds, the multiplicity of goals and the nature of memory processes (see section 5.2.3 for the detailed explanation concerning meme and these factors, which are called behavior shaping factors). The following are specific questions that a CCE study has to deal with for respective behavioral events:

1) Which memes were activated?

2) Under which conditions were the memes activated?

3) How had the meme been formed?

The answers will be analyzed to construct models that explain and predict human beings' behavior in the study field.

5.2.1.2. How to understand

This section discusses what kinds of data are available for deriving answers to the above questions. The origins of the data will be the results of observation of human beings' daily action selection processes in real-world settings instead of in simulated laboratory experimental settings. A list of data that are obtainable with little interference with the participants' activities are as follows:

1) *Behavior observation records*: Investigators will record the participants' behavior without any intervention with their activities.

2) *Behavior measurement records*: Sensors will be attached to the participants to record their physiological activities, e.g. a pin microphone to record their vocalizations, a small ear-mounted camera to record the scene they are viewing, an electrocardiograph to record their physiological responses to the events and so on.

3) *On site self-reports*: Study participants themselves will take photos, brief notes, voice recording, etc., concerning their activities while their memories of the events remain fresh.

4) *Utterances in retrospective interviews*: Behavioral observation records, behavioral measurement records, and on site self-reports will be used to reconstruct their active memes at the time of events by conducting a series of retrospective interviews. Their utterances in the interview sessions will be recorded.

5.2.2. CCE procedure

CCE is carried out in the following six steps as shown in Figure 5.1:

1) *Phase 1 of "preliminary socio-ecological modeling"*: It defines the study field. It is important to specify the study field sufficiently to undertake successful CCE studies. Manifestations of behavior selection shaping factors under the characteristic atmosphere of the study field, which must be

understood in terms of the effects of behavior selection shaping factors, will be observed in the study field.

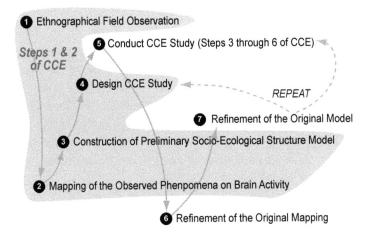

Figure 5.1. *The CCE procedure*

2) *Phase 2 of "preliminary socioecological modeling"*: It defines critical parameters. Critical parameters are initial hypotheses about the behavior selection shaping factors that should work when human beings' activities are organized in the study field. To do this, it is necessary to examine the structure and dynamics of the study field in order to ensure the existence of chronological changes in the people in question, to construct hypotheses about the critical parameters and to carry out a preliminary test. Steps 1 and 2 are conducted interchangeably to define the parameter space to be explored.

3) *Monitor recruiting*: It selects elite monitors. In order to conduct CCE, study participants (elite monitors) are selected. Each point in the parameter space has values, continuous or discrete. The study question is "what such and such people would do in such and such way in such and such circumstance (not an average behavior)". Therefore, elite monitors, such and such persons, are selected by consulting the parameter space. In this process, it is necessary that the points in the parameter space, which correspond to the elite monitors, are appropriate for analyzing the structure and dynamics of the study field. Monitor selection is conducted by purposive sampling rather than by random sampling.

4) *Monitor behavior observation:* It records the monitors' behavior. The elite monitors are expected to behave as they normally do at the study field. Their behavior is recorded in such a way that the collected data are rich enough to consider the results in terms of the parameter space and as unintrusively as circumstances allow.

5) *Individual model construction:* It conducts retrospective interviews. The collected data are used to clarify the structure of the meme of the elite monitors by conducting a series of structured interviews. The results of the interviews are analyzed for the purpose of defining the basis of the representations of the collected data. The analysis involves finding common terms used in the interviews and common activities that are defined by combinations of the common terms, as well as statistical analysis of the activities, e.g. factor analysis and cluster analysis.

6) *Socioecological model construction:* It construct models. The last step of CCE is to construct models that address "such and such people would do what in such and such way in such and such circumstances".

5.2.3. *Behavior selection shaping factors*

CCE studies are carried out by keeping the following critical factors for understanding human beings' daily behavior in mind.

5.2.3.1. *Two Minds*

As described in the introduction, Two Minds is one of the crucial factors for understanding human beings' action selection processes. System 1 of Two Minds corresponds to the A^2BC layer of NDHB-model/RT and System 2 corresponds to the C layer, respectively, as described in section 2.4, and its operation is simulated by MHP/RT, as described in section 2.5. System 1 is a fast feed-forward control process oriented toward immediate action (System 1 before mode), and is experienced passively, outside of conscious awareness (System 1 after mode). In contrast, System 2 is a slow feedback control process oriented toward future action (System 2 before mode), and is experienced actively and consciously (System 2 after mode). There is a huge difference in processing speed between the two systems; rational processing typically takes minutes to hours, whereas experiential processing typically extends from hundreds of milliseconds to tens of seconds (see Figure 2.11). A large part of human beings' daily activities are immediate actions and are therefore under control of System 1. System 2 intervenes with System 1 to better organize the overall outcome of the processing through consciously envisioning possible futures. Human beings' behavior is the outcome of the operation of System 1 and System 2 along the time dimension, which work in parallel and at the same time work in synchronous with the development of the states of the environment. The observed data concerning the study participants' behavior at a study field must be understood from the viewpoint of the operation of Two Minds along the time dimension. Understanding "how" human beings carry out action selection processes in the ever-changing environment should reduce to understanding how the four processing modes of MHP/RT are coordinated in real life situations.

5.2.3.2. *Meme that mediates individuals and society*

Moment-by-moment decision-making and action selection is carried out by utilizing knowledge that is activated from long-term memory in response to the recognized objects that exist in the external world. A meme is an entity that represents the information associated with the object that a person can recognize. Therefore, active memes play a critical role in decision-making and action selection processes. The term "meme", originally coined by Dawkins [DAW 76], was conceptual and not clearly defined. However, meme can be defined more clearly by assuming that meme itself is structured in accord with the structure of living organisms, which is characterized by nonlinear, multilayered information structure.

As described in section 2.3.1, the structured meme consists of the following three nonlinear layers, each of which is associated with multidimensional memory frames described in section 3.1.2:

– action-level memes represent bodily actions, corresponding to PMD, BMD, and MMD;

– behavior-level memes represent behaviors in the environment, corresponding to PMD and RM;

– culture-level memes represent culture, corresponding to PMD and WMD.

Understanding "what" human beings carry out decision-making and action selection processes in the ever-changing environment should reduce to identifying active memes considering functional flow structure and evolving cyclic network structure in the layered structure of multidimensional memory frames as shown in Figure 3.5, while performing actions with MHP/RT, in conjunction with the memorization process as shown in Figure 3.3.

5.2.3.3. *Multiplicity of behavioral goals*

Morris [MOR 06] defined 17 happiness goals. It is assumed that a person pursues one of the 17 goals at every moment, and switches to another when appropriate by evaluating the current circumstances. CCE needs to identify the current goal and elucidate the goal enabling conditions by consulting maximum satisfaction architecture described in section 2.1 working at the B layer of NDHB-model/RT (section 2.4). A person feels satisfaction when a goal is accomplished. The amount of satisfaction felt is influenced by the factors that characterize the shape of trajectory of behavioral outcome. There are six critical factors to make people feel satisfaction (see section 2.1.4 and Figure 2.2).

5.2.3.4. *Usage of memory under strong interaction between environment and behavior*

Memory processes play a crucial role on the course of decision-making and action selection processes and their results, i.e. the behavior he or she ultimately selects and carries out. As Newell [NEW 90] described in his seminal book, *Unified Theories of Cognition*, human beings operate differently according to the characteristic times of the environment they are in (see Figure 2.11). When real-time constraints are strong, slow memory processes, which use long-term memory, should not participate in the whole processing. In other words, only the unconscious side of the Two Minds (System 1) should work. On the contrary, when there are little real-time constraints, both System 1 and System 2, consciousness and unconsciousness systems work collaboratively in some cases and independently in other cases. Memory processes stay in the back of meme activation, and therefore when we want to envision active memes at the specific time when the event occurred, he or she has to take into account the plausible memory processes that should have operated given the time constraint imposed on the participant at that time.

6

A CCE Study: Slow Self-paced Navigation

With the focus of action selection processes involved in slow self-paced navigation, this chapter illustrates a case study that adopted the CCE methodology to investigate how elderly people use guide signs at train stations when they have to transfer lines, in addition to the use of facilities such as restrooms, lockers, elevators, telephones and so on. This study was sponsored by a train company in Japan and had the purpose of gaining insight for improving the usability of guide signs at train stations for elderly passengers (see Figure 6.1 for an example signboard).

6.1. Introduction: navigation in a train station by following signs[1]

We would like to illustrate a train station navigation study to show how an actual CCE study was conducted. We were interested in how elderly passengers use guide signs at railway stations, such as the one shown in Figure 6.1, when they wanted to use facilities, e.g. toilets, coin-operated lockers, etc., or when they had to transfer to another line. In this chapter, the "know the users" problem that this book focuses on is treated as "know the passengers" problem. According to the CCE steps as shown in Figure 5.1, the study was conducted as follows:

– *Step 1:* at first, from the field observations, we realized that cognitive functions such as *planning* for searching something necessary at train stations, *attention* for selectively focusing on task relevant information from the environment and *working memory* for keeping the task relevant information active for performing actions smoothly are critical functions for understanding passengers' behavior.

---

1 This chapter is from [KIT 12a].

– *Steps 2 and 3:* we conducted simulations by mapping these cognitive functions on MHP/RT, as shown in Figure 2.10, and derived ideas for a field study; on the one hand, people who do not have any problems in these cognitive functions would perform navigation tasks at train stations smoothly; on the other hand, people who have any problems in these cognitive functions would show some problems.

– *Step 4:* then, we designed a CCE study in which we would attempt to understand what people who do not have sufficient level of attention, for example, would do to accomplish the task of searching for a toilet, for instance.

– *Step 5:* we selected 12 study participants from 168 elderly people based on their scores of paper-based cognitive ability assessment tests; for example, three study participants had poor attention but had no problem in planning and working memory.

The following sections describe in detail how the CCE study was conducted.

Figure 6.1. *Signboard at the Tokyo station*

6.2. Steps 1 and 2 of CCE

The study field was a train station. The target activity was to navigate the train station on foot by using signs without asking help from others for directions. Elderly people's navigation behavior was to be investigated. The study question was "what would such and such elderly people do for carrying out navigation missions at train stations by using sign boards?"

Navigating the station smoothly requires not only physical actions but also cognitive and behavioral abilities, including the following activities:

1) determine a target appropriate to the purpose;

2) search for the target;

3) reach the target;

4) achieve the missions.

It was assumed that the following four cognitive abilities are indispensable for elderly people to accomplish navigation missions at train stations (1) attention, (2) working memory, and (3) planning, which are known to decrease independently with age, and (4) experience of using the train station. These constitute the critical parameters.

6.2.1. *Attention, planning and working memory*

As will be described in section 6.2.2, Kitajima and Toyota [KIT 12a] provide theoretically motivated accounts of these cognitive functions that serve as critical parameters, which essentially validate the selection of the critical parameters for this study that were carried out on the basis of general psychological considerations. Brief descriptions for these cognitive abilities are as follows:

– *Attention:* the ability to distinguish information pertinent to the task at hand from extraneous noises. Although the ability to separate target information from external noises plays an important role in daily behavior, it is known that aging makes it difficult to ignore such unrelated information, resulting in a delay in discovering the target information. As the result, signs may be overlooked in one's daily life.

– *Planning:* the prioritization and sequential implementation of the steps necessary to achieve a goal. It consists of repetitive cycles of appropriately setting a lower level goal required to achieve the current goal, maintaining the lower level goal until it is achieved, and when that goal has been achieved, then setting the next new lower level goal.

– *Working memory:* refers to a psychological system that both stores information briefly and allows manipulation and use of the stored information. This function is the basis of the complex cognitive activities performed by a person. However, working memory has a basic limitation: it can hold only a limited amount of information at one time. Due to this limitation, a person with an impaired working memory function is likely to lose the original goal and necessary information for a given action and hence fail to accomplish all the goals necessary to accomplish the task.

6.2.2. *An MHP/RT simulation of navigation behavior*[2]

In this section, we illustrate how MHP/RT simulates navigation behavior by taking wayfinding at a train station for a concrete example. We focus specifically on how the various components of MHP/RT, as shown in Figure 2.10, *should* work coherently and interactively to show organized navigation behavior. System 1, that controls automatic behavior, and System 2, that monitors operations of System 1 and controls conscious decision-making, need to work jointly to behave synchronously with the ever-changing environment that changes as the agent changes its states.

6.2.2.1. *Specification of navigation behavior to be simulated*

In order to run an MHP/RT simulation, we need to specify conditions that may affect its working. We start from a general condition and then elaborate it to derive detailed conditions by taking into account the specific situations we are interested in.

6.2.2.1.1. Higher level description of navigation behavior

At the highest level, the behavior we focus on is described as follows:

A person reaches his/her destinations where he/she can accomplish his/her tasks by having transfer his/her body all by him/herself according to his/her decisions, which are made by utilizing information from the environment.

To elaborate the above description, we take "train station" as an instance of the environment, and "a person who has experience of utilizing train stations" as an instance of "a person". The destinations will be concrete objects at the train station, such as a platform from which to take a train, a locker in which to store bags and so on. The person has to accomplish the task all by him/herself without asking for help.

6.2.2.1.2. Preparation for simulating navigation behavior

We try to derive the description of navigation situation detailed enough for MHP/RT to operate on.

---

2 The description of this section is adapted from section 3 of our article [KIT 12a].

Let us start with the environment. A train station is a complex of facilities centered on platforms where trains arrive and depart. The facilities include shops, waiting rooms, stairs, elevators, ticketing machines, restrooms, lockers and so on. Each facility can become the destination of navigation in the train station. Each facility has its distinctive appearance and is therefore easy for a person to recognize at a first glance.

Next, we consider the nature of a person who navigates in a train station. A task such as "to use a facility" is accomplished by reaching the place where the facility is, or a task "to take a specific train" is accomplished by reaching the platform that the train leaves from. In order to reach the destinations, a person navigates the train station on foot, or uses alternative methods such as escalators or elevators. These movements define the boundary conditions of navigation behavior such as the rate of change in information from the environment, the rate of decision-making and the length of time allowed to make decisions, which are characterized by "slow navigation behavior".

A person as described above navigates a train station as described above. Navigation behavior is represented by a series of geographical coordinates:

$$\{\cdots, P(T(-1)), P(T(0))\}$$

where $T(-N)$ denotes the time when a decision was made, either consciously or unconsciously, concerning how to navigate a place $P(T(-N))$. $T(0)$ denotes the time the last decision was made. In addition, $P(T(-(N-1))) \neq P(T(-N))$, namely, the person does not stay at one place. The interval between two successive decision-making events depends on the situation. And the duration that each decision-making required is not necessarily equal to $T(-N) - T(-(N-1))$; it could be shorter in some cases or longer in other cases. As the result of decision-making at the place $P(T(0))$, the person moves to the next place $P(T(1))$. The decision at $P(T(0))$ is influenced by the past decisions, $P(T(-N))$, where $N = 1, 2, \cdots, N_s$ and N_s is the time when the person started navigation in the train station.

6.2.2.2. MHP/RT simulation

Now, we can identify the components of MHP/RT, as shown in Figure 2.10, that should affect the decision-making process at $P(T(0))$, with the help of a more general description of MHP/RT, as shown in Figure 2.9. The components are listed as follows:

– *Sensory information filter:* how the *physically* available information at place P is actually input in System 1, System 2, and memory;

– *Resonance:* what kind of knowledge might resonate with the input information;

– *Feedback from consciousness:* how the resonated knowledge should affect the future processes of input of information from the environment or functioning of System 2 before modes;

– *Frame rate:* the rate of decision-making, ranging from 100 to 10s corresponding to the range of the cognitive band in Figure 2.11.

At this point, we can assume that the performance of the above four components, high versus low, should affect the overall performance of a person's navigation behavior. In the following sections, we discuss in more detail how the differences in the performance of each component should affect navigation behavior.

6.2.2.2.1. Sensory information filter

Sensory information filters work at the interface between System 1, System 2 and memory, and the physical world that is constructed by a number of physical objects. A large part of information originates from the visual and auditory stimuli emitted from the physical objects. System 1, System 2 and memory acquire these kinds of information through the sensory information filter and construct cognitive objects, i.e. representations of the physical objects that are manipulable by System 1, System 2 and memory. The working of the sensory information filter is otherwise called *attention*. What should happen for a person who has a low attention function? Due to attention deficiency, this person should have difficulty in constructing appropriate cognitive objects. This happens even if he/she has appropriate feedback from consciousness. As the result, he/she should activate knowledge that resonates with the inappropriate cognitive objects, and he/she should have inappropriate feedback from consciousness that is related with the inappropriately activated knowledge. It should be difficult for this person to perform effective actions for attaining the behavioral goals.

6.2.2.2.2. Resonance

Resonance occurs between cognitive objects and memory, or knowledge stored in long-term memory. The necessary condition for strong resonance to happen is the presence of active meme in long-term memory (LTM). Meme refers to a fragment of knowledge in LTM that has the potential to resonate with cognitive objects in working memory. In general, a construct that includes active memes as its components is called *mental model*. The cognitive objects created at the place P, or the active cognitive objects, are likely to activate various kinds of mental models that include similar cognitive objects to the active memes. One kind of mental model concerns action sequences and the other concerns structures of train stations that are related with the active cognitive objects. Furthermore, the components of activated mental models are likely to activate more. Cognitive objects that are included in the activated action sequences can activate parts of structure of train stations. Cognitive objects that are included in the activated structure can activate action sequences that are related to the activated structure. In other words, once strong resonance occurs, it is likely that a wide range of knowledge is activated, which is not restricted to knowledge directly related to the current situation.

6.2.2.2.3. Feedback from consciousness

Feedback from consciousness, or functioning of System 2 before mode, affects future decision-making events. This function is called *planning*. It operates the sensory information filter by utilizing activated knowledge. A person who has strong feedback from consciousness can obtain strong representations concerning future events that are likely to happen, and can prepare an effective sensory information filter that is affected by the feedback. When a person behaves automatically under the control of System 1, or he/she is under System 1 before mode, feedback from consciousness does not work. However, once System 2 takes control, possibly because of a breakdown of the operation of System 1, the person is led to the behavioral mode of conscious decision-making. The results of the decision-making of a person with high feedback from consciousness appear farsighted. On the contrary, those of a person with low feedback from consciousness appear aimless or short-sighted even when he/she has activated appropriate knowledge.

6.2.2.2.4. Frame Rate

A compound that consists of the cognitive objects and their resonance forms a cognitive frame that interfaces System 1 and System 2, which in effect serves as so-called *working memory*. System 2 uses the representation of cognitive frame to activate relevant knowledge for preparation of future events. System 1 uses it for controlling attention. Cognitive frame is updated less frequently as far as behavior is conducted automatically, i.e. System 1 controls behavior. System 2 monitors whether the circumstances in System 1 change as expected. On the other hand, cognitive frame is updated more frequently as the frequency of interventions from System 2 increases, i.e. the person needs to evaluate the change in circumstances carefully to behave appropriately. If a person cannot update frames frequently enough to follow the change in circumstances, it appears that he/she has based their decisions on narrow alternatives. Therefore, the ability to set the frame rate as high as needed should affect the result of behavior.

6.3. Step 3 of CCE: monitor recruiting

The critical parameters for the CCE study were the cognitive functions, attention, working memory, and planning, and the experience of using the train stations where the study would be conducted. Each of the four critical parameters has values, normal or weak (presence or absence in the case of experience), and the parameter spaces to explore are defined by their combinations. We were interested in studying how individual parameters would affect navigation behavior; we took the lesion approach to compare behavior of participants who had the value "weak" for one parameter and "normal" for the other three parameters with that of participants who had no "weak" values. It was straightforward to estimate presence/absence of experience. The following method was used to estimate normal/weak concerning the three cognitive functions.

6.3.1. *Investigation of cognitive aging characteristics*

To investigate cognitive aging characteristics, we designed a cognitive function study using the AIST cognitive aging study [SUT 10] as the base, modified the contents of the study according to the contents of our current study and then conducted a survey. This study was devised so that the participants' knowledge and/or general memory loss did not affect the study results. Table 6.1 presents the study items for examining characteristics of cognitive functions.

Cognitive function	Study item
Attention	Search for target images
	Select correct shape/figure with designated feature
Working memory	Write mirrored characters
	Write words in reverse
Planning	Recall and write a sequence of daily actions

Table 6.1. *Study items for cognitive functions*

We conducted two studies by changing monitor selection conditions. Participants in the first study were 168 elderly people registered with the Silver Human Resource Center located in the Tokyo metropolitan area. The second study included 154 elderly people. Table 6.2 presents the results.

Ability in cognitive functions	%
First study	
Normal ability in all functions	4.7
Inferior in only one of the functions	40.4
Inferior attention (only)	8.3
Inferior working memory (only)	8.9
Inferior planning (only)	23.2
Second study	
Normal in only one of the functions	17.6
Normal attention (only)	6.5
Normal working memory (only)	7.1
Normal planning (only)	4.0

Table 6.2. *Results of the cognitive aging survey*

6.4. Steps 4 and 5 of CCE: monitor behavior observation and individual model construction

To identify the cognitive and behavioral processes of elderly people's navigation through a train station, we conducted surveys of actual behavior at JR East stations in the Tokyo metropolitan area.

Two field surveys were conducted. In the first survey, based on their scores of the paper-based cognitive ability assessment tests, four groups were defined:

one with no problem and the other three with one inferior cognitive function. All groups had no experience of using the train stations where the surveys were conducted for the past 10 years. Each of three participants from each group performed tasks, such as transferring from line A to line B and using facilities at train stations, at one of three stations (Akihabara, Ohmiya and Sugamo). In the second survey, a total of 154 elderly participants took the paper tests, and three groups, each of which had one normal cognitive function, were defined. Three from each group with different use experience performed tasks at two stations (Tokyo and Shibuya).

6.4.1. Train stations, tasks and participants

For the first study, we selected three stations that have different structures. This was done for the purpose of discovering factors affecting behavior that are independent of the structure of the station and are peculiar to the cognitive function characteristics of each participant, with a focus on planning, attention and working memory. In Table 6.3, we describe briefly the features of the selected train stations and the assigned tasks at each station. We selected 12 participants, three participants from each of four groups: one group of those with normal ability in all functions and three groups of those with inferior ability in one of the cognitive functions. Four participants with different cognitive aging characteristics performed the task at each of the three stations.

For the second study, we specifically focused on the effect of the presence or absence of experience with using the train stations at the study sites on the participants' navigation behavior. We selected two train stations, Tokyo and Shibuya, in the Tokyo metropolitan area, and selected three participants for each station who had only one normal cognitive function. One of these participants had recently used the Tokyo station but not the Shibuya station, one had recently used the Shibuya station but had not used the Tokyo station and the other had never used either station. Therefore, we selected a total of nine participants. The tasks involved reaching designated destinations. Since we were interested in the effect of experience and related mental models of the structure of the station, rather than the mental model of the procedure, we set the task route to be longer and wider than the ones for the first study, which focused more on navigation by following signboards.

Station	Akihabara station	Sugamo station	Ohmiya station
Feature	Platforms on two stories cross each other	Simple structure with an island-type platform	Has four stories for the Shinkansen, concourse and conventional lines accompanied by a wide space
Main task	Change trains by moving from the No. 1 or No. 2 platform for the Yamanote/Keihin-Tohoku line to the No. 5 platform for the Sobu line for Shinjuku	(1) Move from the platform for the Togenuki Jizo and (2) move from the arcade to the Sugamo station and take a train for Mejiro	Move from the east entrance to the platform for the Saikyo line and take a train for Ikebuturo
Subtasks	– Use the toilet – Use a telephone	– Use the toilet – Buy a ticket – Use a coin locker (deposit and retrieve) – Use an elevator	– Use the toilet – Buy a ticket – Use a coin locker (deposit and retrieve)

Table 6.3. *Brief description of the features of the selected train stations and the assigned tasks at each station*

6.4.2. *Method*

The task was instructed to each participant, whose behavior was recorded using a small wireless pinhole CMOS camera attached to the participant's hat, a wireless microphone and a whole back view CCD camera (Figure 6.2, left and center). Immediately after each task, the participants were taken into a room and interviewed for their background knowledge and explanation of their behavior while reviewing the recorded videos (Figure 6.2, right).

Figure 6.2. *Left: participant performing a task at the Sugamo station; center: the equipment; right: interview after task*

The tasks involved searching to find the place in which to perform the tasks. We were interested in representing the participants' behavior in terms of state transitions in the problem space. Therefore, by comprehensively considering the video recording and the results of the interviews, we divided a series of actions into segments, each consisting of a searching action, and further described them in detail using the following five items:

1) goal;

2) movement and behavior observed;

3) motivation and the object of searching;

4) guide boards and signs referred to, and

5) attributes of referral, i.e. collection of information or confirmation.

6.5. Step 6 of CCE: socioecological model construction

The result was then examined from the viewpoint of the cognitive characteristics of each participant. The results essentially indicated the following:

– persons with inferior planning function but with normal attention function did not use the guide signs when they had a mental model; however, they did not gather task-relevant information but instead gathered irrelevant information when they had no mental model, because of the lack of definite task goals, causing them to get lost.

– persons with inferior planning function and inferior attention consistently had difficulty gathering task-relevant information by using guide signs because of the vague description of behavioral goals.

Although the conventional guideline for the elderly is based on the presumption that the elderly people will look at signs, the results suggested that such a supposition is not always true. We believe this gives us an important clue to solving usability problems at train stations. For the inferior attention group, for example, it will be useful to provide appropriate symbolic images. For the inferior planning group, on the other hand, individual guides will be necessary.

6.6. Discussion

This section derives implications for navigation in a virtual environment (e.g. web navigation).

6.6.1. *Two modes of navigation*

Suppose a person is placed in an environment that he/she has never visited and given a navigation mission that is familiar to him/her. He/she can anticipate the goal state and imagine the problem space that should extend as he/she proceeds. The representation could be very detailed or not, depending on his/her knowledge of this situation. It is suggested that in this situation, two qualitatively different modes of navigation processes exist. The first is "anticipation-based navigation" in which "feedback from consciousness" in MHP/RT works effectively. The second is "event-based navigation" in which feedback does not work, and moment-by-moment decision-making and action selection is required. The distinction between anticipation-based action and event-based action is not new in the study of goal-directed human behavior. For example, it was studied in the field of human–machine interaction when display-based interaction became popular in the 1990s; Payne [PAY 91] compared "plan-based" action and "display-based" action with the focus of the role of information flow from device to user in skilled activity in human–machine interaction. This section provides a coherent account for these two modes from the viewpoint of MHP/RT's operations.

6.6.1.1. *Anticipation-based navigation*

Even if the environment is new to the participant, the mission is familiar to him/her. Therefore, when starting the mission, he/she is able to activate mental models associated with the mission. If the level of the representation of the mental model is appropriate for the sensory information filter to function effectively in the environment, it is possible for him/her to input information from the environment as specified by the mental model. The mental model may be one for procedures (i.e. know-how) or one for objects in the environment (i.e. know-that). The input information resonates with the knowledge in LTM and updates the representation of the active mental models to be used to create feedback from consciousness. The feedback forms anticipation concerning the future development of the person and the environment. While this cycle continues as the person navigates, it is said that the person is navigating in the mode of anticipation-based navigation. In this mode, System 2 monitors the operation of System 1 and intervenes when a large discrepancy exists between the anticipation concerning the situation to come next and the actual situation. However, the intervention does not last long, and System 1 immediately reverts to the anticipation-based navigation cycle.

6.6.1.2. *Event-based navigation*

When anticipation-based navigation seriously breaks down, the participant is forced to switch to the event-based navigation mode in order to continue the mission. Breakdown can occur when the initial mental model is found to be inappropriate: (1) the level of representation is appropriate, but the sensory information filter that reflects feedback from consciousness does not work because of a serious discrepancy between the representation of the filter and the actual environment (i.e. the filter does not work at all), or (2) the level of representation is not detailed enough for consciously defining the sensory information filter. A person who is in the event-based navigation mode must monitor the progress more frequently than one who is in the anticipation-based navigation mode, and must select the next action within the time allowed by deliberate processing. Therefore, the action selection process in this situation looks like obeying the satisficing principle defined by Simon [SIM 56] and the speed-accuracy tradeoff applies. In this mode, System 2 takes control of navigation behavior. Event-based navigation can switch to anticipation-based navigation once the cycle is reestablished, including such processes as starting with feedback from consciousness, sensory information filter, resonance with LTM and ending with updating feedback from consciousness.

6.6.2. *Web navigation*

Web navigation is defined by the process of reaching a target page where the user is searching for the information, provided from a start page, by successively selecting hyperlinks to initiate a transition from the current page to the next page. A number of cognitive models simulate users who navigate the Web in search of information to be found on the target page. However, these cognitive models are not designed to simulate user behavior along the time dimension; therefore, they are qualitatively different from the architecture model MHP/RT. It would be worthwhile, however, to position the existing cognitive models from the viewpoint of MHP/RT's navigation modes just described.

The comprehension-based linked model of deliberate search (CoLiDeS) [KIT 00] simulates users searching for information on the Web by successively selecting hyperlinks until they reach content pages that provide the information they are seeking (i.e. target pages). The core mechanism consists of the following two processes:

1) selecting a region on a Web page in which a hyperlink directed toward the content pages is expected to be found;

2) selecting the hyperlink in that region that is most likely to lead to the target pages.

CoLiDeS is built on Kintsch's construction–integration theory of text comprehension [KIN 88, KIN 98]. CoLiDeS is capable of simulating a mode of Web navigation that is best conceived as a process analogous to comprehending text for gaining coherent understanding of a document. In other words, it simulates fast feed-forward processing of textual information on a Web page for selecting a hyperlink that is most consistent with the current goal. Therefore, CoLiDeS basically models anticipation-based navigation, mainly by System 1, or MHP/RT's Mode 1 operation.

CoLiDeS does not simulate all aspects of Web navigation, only goal-directed forward search. Indeed, CoLiDeS does not backtrack when it encounters impasses, unlike SNIF-ACT [FU 07], which was built on the Adaptive Control of Thought Rationa (ACT-R) cognitive architecture [AND 93, AND 07] and is capable of simulating both forward search and backtracking. CoLiDeS does not change the initial set of search keywords when it turns out to be inappropriate, and it does not simulate such activities as collecting Web pages that are relevant to a certain topic by judging the relevance of retrieved Web pages. The deliberate processes, including backtracking, are event-based navigation processes in which anticipation does not work. They are performed mainly by System 2 and can be modeled by MHP/RT's Mode 2 operation.

6.6.3. *Nature of complicated navigation processes*

Web navigation can be regarded as the interleaving of Mode 1 and Mode 2 of MHP/RT operation modes. When the information to search is well specified, the ideal operational mode is Mode 1 (i.e. no serious backtracking should occur). Mode 1 is realized by anticipation-based navigation. In many cases, it is difficult for a person to anticipate the next situation by resorting solely to his/her knowledge because remembering intermediate steps for operating graphical interface is not easy [PAY 91] and Web contents are too unstable to remember. A number of ideas have been developed that essentially support the person in intellectual anticipation. For example, Olston and Chi [OLS 03] proposed the ScentTrail system for searching and browsing a Web site. ScentTrail modifies the rendering of links to enhance information scent cues that are particularly useful, given users' goals. Previews associated with search results are provided by a number of search engines (e.g. "instant preview" by Google and "hover preview" by Bing). They should help the user construct useful anticipation as to where each search result will take him/her before actually transitioning into it. MHP/RT also carries out processes of dealing with previews, which are another source of information to be integrated with the results of just completed processes.

6.7. Conclusions

The observational study at train stations indicated that participants manifest behavior that reflects their covert processes. However, we should bear in mind that overtly similar behavior manifests from totally different covert processes. For example, it was observed that two participants got lost in the same situation from two different covert processes (one person had a deficit in the planning function, and the other had a deficit in the attention function). The normal group could carry out the tasks at stations in the anticipation-based navigation mode. However, individuals with problems in cognitive functions easily broke down and had to operate in the event-based navigation mode. A breakdown can easily occur under strong time constraints. This is because time constraints tend to increase the processing demands, so that synchronization between the ever-changing environment and the agent is established less flexibly. Individual differences in terms of the performance of cognitive functions were clearly observed as time constraints become stronger.

The processes of navigation are complicated. However, simulating these processes along the time dimension can provide us with an appropriate understanding of the interaction between the ever-changing environment and an actively and autonomously behaving agent.

7

Fast Externally-paced Navigation

With the focus of action selection processes involved in fast externally-paced navigation, this chapter illustrates a case study that adopted the CCE methodology to derive information necessary for safe and enjoyable driving for drivers while driving. Note that this is a time-critical situation where System 2 before mode and System 1 before mode should be appropriately coordinated along the information provided externally, e.g. through a car navigation system of a human navigator. The study was designed in such a way that participants as drivers should perform event-based navigation, and have aided to conduct otherwise impossible driving in System 2 before mode, i.e. anticipation-based navigation, by "timely" provided "appropriate" information.

7.1. Introduction[1]

The primary purpose of driving is to transfer persons or things from one place to another. The primary mission of the driver is to control the vehicle safely. This may include the achievement of objectives such as energy efficiency, punctuality and so forth, as optional missions. Traditional car navigation systems are expected to provide information that helps drivers to accomplish their mission of maneuvering satisfactorily. However, with the advent of telematics, modern car navigation systems have begun providing location-based information, such as recommendations of local restaurants along the route. The infrastructure enabling the provision of location-based and context-sensitive information is being developed, making it possible to provide information to drivers that would allow them to experience more safe and enjoyable driving in terms of not only the maneuvering mission but also a variety of concerns encountered en route.

---

1 This chapter is from [KIT 09].

Technological development is very rapid, and it will be possible in the near future to provide information that is necessary for drivers in order to make driving safe and enjoyable. However, what is lacking at the moment is knowledge concerning what information is actually needed by drivers. Due to this problem, the provision of information by the modern car navigation systems is not completely appropriate. In other words, "know the drivers" is the key issue. "Drivers" are considered as "users" to be understood in this chapter. In some cases, the content of the provided information is not what the drivers actually need, and therefore it may be evaluated as annoying. In other cases, the information is not provided in a form that the driver can easily understand, e.g. the driver may prefer "distance to the intersection to turn" over "the number of blocks to the intersection to turn".

This chapter describes a series of on-road observations conducted as a CCE study for elucidating the nature of information that drivers consider necessary to make driving safe and enjoyable. This knowledge should provide a basis for designing an information-provision service for safe and enjoyable driving. A list of such information based on the results of the on-road observations are identified. Some kinds of information can be easily provided by applying currently available or developing technology, whereas other kinds will require extensive technological development.

Similar to the procedure discussed in Chapter 6 and according to the CCE steps as shown in Figure 5.1 (Chapter 5), the study was conducted as follows:

– *Step 1*: navigational characteristics similar to the characteristics discussed in Chapter 6 were obtained from the field observations, i.e. such cognitive functions as *planning* for foreseeing future driving routes and road conditions, *attention* for selectively focusing on objects necessary for safety driving in the environment, and *working memory* for keeping the task relevant information active for performing safe and enjoyable driving.

– *Steps 2 and 3:* we conducted simulations by mapping these cognitive functions on MHP/RT as shown in Figure 2.10, and derived ideas for a field study; three kinds of information for safe and enjoyable driving were identified:

1) guidance for routing;

2) support for safe driving;

3) provision of miscellaneous information, such as information about daily topics of interest to the driver and information about interesting things to see along the route.

– *Step 4:* then, we designed a CCE study in which four pairs of participants were chosen from among those responding to a Web survey and attending a follow-up interview.

– *Step 5:* each pair was asked to drive along six routes. Three of the routes were familiar to one of the pair and new to the other, with the former serving as navigator and the latter serving as driver. For the other three routes, the roles were reversed. Three interviews were conducted, one coming after two drives in which the pair played both roles in order to derive information considered necessary for safe and enjoyable driving by the participants who served as drivers on the routes unknown to them.

7.2. Steps 1 and 2 of CCE

Navigation means "going from one place to another", where "place" could be either a physical place in the four-dimensional universe or a virtual place in informational space. Navigation could be either fast or slow in comparison with the characteristic times of human action as specified by Newell's time scale of action (Figure 2.11). As mentioned in Chapter 6, navigation speed is at the order of walking speed, i.e. 4–5 km/hr, whereas in this chapter, it is about at the order of driving speed, i.e. 30–100 km/hr. However, the analysis described in section 6.2 is still valid even if the characteristic speed is faster for driving. Therefore, even in the case of driving, the following cognitive functions described in section 6.2.1 are considered as important while driving:

– attention;

– planning;

– working memory.

An MHP/RT simulation of driver behavior is similar to the one mentioned in section 6.2.2 because the same cognitive functions are assumed to affect behavior of drivers. Therefore, the following four components of MHP/RT should have effect on the detailed performance of drivers:

– sensory information filter;

– resonance;

– feedback from consciousness;

– frame rate.

7.2.1. *Designing a CCE study*

The focus of this study is how the processes described in Figure 2.10 should become smoother when some information is provided to the driver who cannot otherwise deal with the driving situation smoothly. In other words, identification of conditions of externally provided information that goes through sensory information filter and resonate with the driver's memory to help create appropriate feedback from consciousness within the range of frame rate of update of working memory, which is used for other on-going processes for driving. The three cognitive functions need to be coordinated appropriately in the ever-changing driving environment when such information is provided in context:

1) guidance for routing;

2) support for safe driving;

3) provision of miscellaneous information, such as information about daily topics of interest to the driver and information about interesting things to see along the route.

This requires special considerations when designing a CCE study, which is very different from the one described in Chapter 6 for slow self-paced navigation, where little coordination among cognitive functions was necessary, or timeliness and appropriateness of external information should not have had large effects on the passengers' behavior.

7.2.1.1. *Outline of the study*

We need to conduct a series of on-road observations to extract information necessary for safe and enjoyable driving. A number of pairs of participants, say four pairs, join the study. The two persons in each pair should be acquainted with each other very well and know each other's driving attitude and knowledge about driving, so they are expected to provide information necessary for safe and enjoyable driving to the driver when their partner is driving along an unfamiliar route.

Each pair will participate in three sessions with different purposes. Each session consists of a set of two on-road drives with driving times ranging from 30 to 90 min, followed by an interview. The purpose of the interview is to determine the information needed for safe and enjoyable driving. Each drive is videotaped using two digital video cameras as shown in Figure 7.1: one for the outside view (camera B), and the other for the driver and navigator view (camera A).

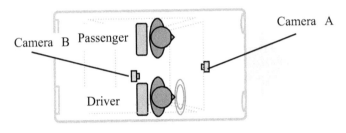

Figure 7.1. *Experimental setup (adapted from [KIT 09])*

7.2.1.1.1. First session: know each other

In the first drive of the first session, one member of the pair drives a route that his/her partner is completely familiar with. The partner thus serves as a human navigator who is expected to provide information that will help the driver to make the journey safe and enjoyable. In the second drive in the first session, the roles are reversed, that is the person who drives in the first drive serves as the navigator, and vice versa. The navigator is expected to provide information necessary for safe and enjoyable driving to the partner, i.e. the driver, by imagining that he or she, the navigator, is driving his/her familiar route and estimating the degree of necessity of provision of information to the driver who is not familiar with the route using his or her own criteria. However, since the navigator does not know exactly what information is actually needed by the driver, some information would not be perceived as necessary by the driver. Therefore, the purpose of the first session is to "know each other better in order to provide information that is actually necessary for safe and enjoyable driving". An interview session conducted immediately after the two drives is designed to facilitate this "know each other" learning. However, the learning is case-based. Thus, the acquired knowledge should not be general enough to be applied to similar situations that do not exactly match the learned knowledge.

7.2.1.1.2. Second session: use case-based knowledge for providing useful information

As the result of the first session, the navigators are expected to have acquired case-based knowledge as to which information should have been perceived by the drivers as necessary for safe and enjoyable driving. The second session asks the navigators to utilize this set of knowledge. As per the first session, one participant serves as a driver in the first drive in the second session and as a navigator in the second drive in the second session, another vice versa. In the interview session, after two drives, their driving behavior is reviewed. This experience should help the navigators to strengthen their case-based knowledge that has been acquired in the first session by using it in the second session. In addition, during the interview session, the navigators are provided with a list of generalized information that are derived by analyzing the instances in the drives in the first and second sessions when information is needed for safe and enjoyable driving. For example, a concrete instruction "turn right at the second traffic light" could be generalized to an expression such as "use traffic lights or landmarks when instructing".

7.2.1.1.3. Third session: use general knowledge for providing useful information

As the result of the second session, the lists of generalized information are handed to the navigators in order to make sure that the listed information would be provided to the drivers when necessary. Two drives follow for each pair of participants exactly same as the first and second sessions.

7.3. Step 3 of CCE: monitor recruiting

The study was conducted from October 2007 to February 2008. It was crucial for this study to recruit participants who were good at providing information for safe and enjoyable driving to the driver. In other words, a person, serving as a navigator for his/her familiar route, has to be able to:

1) simulate a driver's mental processes while he/she is driving an unfamiliar route;

2) find situations where the driver may have some difficulty in deciding what to do while driving;

3) compose appropriate guidance for him/her considering his/her preference to the way in which it is provided;

4) provide it in a timely manner considering the driving and traffic situations.

Therefore, we adopted a two-stage recruiting process consisting of a Web questionnaire for screening and an interview for the final selection.

7.3.1. *Screening*

Questionnaires were distributed to 1,655 individuals who met the following conditions:

1) He/she lives in the metropolitan area of Tokyo;

2) His/her age is between 20 and 50 years;

3) He/she drives his/her car more than twice a month.

Some questions requested them to self-estimate their skill in providing the information necessary for safe and enjoyable driving, such as:

– are you an officious person?

– are you an industrious person?

– are you a considerate person?

A respondent was asked to accompany a person who would participate in the driving sessions. He/she answered these questions on behalf of his/her partner.

The responses were analyzed to select candidate pairs for the on-road observational study. The judgment criterion was whether both the respondent and his/her partner would be able to provide information that was necessary for safe and enjoyable driving while one of them was navigating and the other was driving. Note that both members of the pair would play the roles of navigator and driver. Thus, each was expected to be a good information provider for the other. Ten pairs were selected as candidates for the on-road observations, then further examined in an interview, described below, for the final selection.

7.3.2. *Interview for the final selection*

There were several stages in the interview. First, the answers provided by the respondents were reviewed for their appropriateness. Each candidate pair was then asked to plan the routes for the three driving sessions. A total of six routes were provided. A requirement for each route was that the route was completely familiar to the navigator and yet was new to the driver. In addition, it was anticipated that there would be a number of opportunities for the navigator to provide information necessary for safe and enjoyable driving. During the interview, the candidate pairs were asked to draw the routes on a board. The drawings were used to examine the appropriateness of the routes for this study with a face-to-face interview. An example drawing is shown in Figure 7.2.

 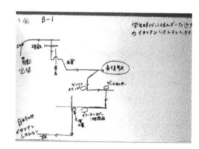

Figure 7.2. *An example of route sketched by a participant*

Following the examination of the responses of the candidate pairs, four pairs were selected for the on-road observational study. Three of the four pairs were married couples, and one was a pair of female colleagues who worked at the same company.

7.4. Steps 4 and 5 of CCE: monitor behavior observation and individual model construction

7.4.1. *Data analysis*

A total of 24 maneuvers were videotaped and analyzed in order to derive the information provided by the navigators to the drivers. As a result, a total of 1,859 information sets were extracted.

7.4.1.1. *Data coding*

Each information set was represented using the following four descriptors:

1) The utterance;

2) The way the information was provided including the timing, and the way the direction was described;

3) The traffic conditions, such as the width of road, speed of the vehicle, etc.;

4) The driver's condition, such as the workload of driving or any preexisting knowledge of the route. The former was estimated by viewing the video and the latter was inferred during the interviews.

7.4.1.2. *Evaluation of the provided information*

In the interviews, each information set was evaluated by the driver as to whether it was effective in helping him/her to conduct safe and enjoyable driving. In addition, likely rationales for the evaluations were attached when possible. In other words, the information provided by the navigator, who judged it should be helpful for the driver based on the result of his/her simulation of driver's mental processes at the time of provision of the information, was examined whether it had been as such by the driver. The accuracy of the simulation was examined and revised if necessary.

However, in reality, it was not possible to allocate enough time to review all of the information, so parts of the provided information were not reviewed thoroughly. We evaluated such information by ranking them at one of the following levels with the help of "simulation model of the driver" as we derived from the interview session:

1) The information was judged as good because it seemed necessary for the driver to conduct safe and enjoyable driving.

2) The information was judged as average because it was not likely to have affected the driver's behavior.

3) The information was judged as poor because it seemed that the driver responded negatively.

7.4.2. *Information necessary for safe and enjoyable driving*

Items evaluated as good were extracted from the whole set of provided information and further classified into three categories:

1) Guidance for routing.

2) Support for safe driving.

3) Provision of miscellaneous information.

In the following, the subcategories of these categories will be described in detail.

7.4.2.1. *Category 1: guidance for routing*

There are nine subcategories under this category as follows:

1) Information that specified the point of action by using an easy-to-understand references for the driver (see section 7.4.3.1 for a detailed example).

2) Information that was useful in planning future actions.

3) Information whose expression was crafted by selecting words that were comprehensible to the driver.

4) Information that augmented the driver's knowledge about the route.

5) Information that specified a route that the driver preferred.

6) Suggestions of drop-by places made by considering the driver's condition.

7) Suggestions of parking places that made the activities undertaken after getting out of the car easier.

8) Timely provision of information that made the driver feel comfortable and relieved.

9) Information that confirmed an action that the driver had carried out according to the navigator's directions.

7.4.2.2. *Category 2: support for safe driving*

There are seven subcategories under this category as follows:

1) Information that helped the driver to resolve undecided situations, leading to safe driving.

2) Information that caused the driver to pay attention to events for safe driving (see section 7.4.3.2 for a detailed example).

3) Information that helped the driver prepare for future actions, ensuring safe and smooth driving (see section 7.4.3.3 for a detailed example).

4) Actions carried out by the navigator that otherwise would have had to have been carried out by the driver.

5) Checks for traffic conditions carried out by the navigator that otherwise would have had to have been carried out by the driver.

6) Pointing out actions missed by the driver.

7) Reflections on improvements in driving behavior.

7.4.2.3. *Category 3: provision of miscellaneous information*

There are two subcategories under this category as follows:

1) Information about daily topics of interest to the driver.

2) Information about interesting things seen along the route (see section 7.4.3.4 for a detailed example).

7.4.3. **Examples**

In this section, four episodes involving the provision of information that was perceived by the driver as necessary information for safe and enjoyable driving will be demonstrated.

7.4.3.1. *Episode 1*

Information which specified the point of action by using an easy-to-understand reference for the driver (see Figure 7.3) was estimated as helpful information. When there was a leading vehicle, the navigator provided routing information by using the leading vehicle as the reference. The area where this guidance was provided had a number of traffic lights and intersections. Therefore, it was not easy for the first-time driver to identify the exact location to make a turn. Thus, this information was evaluated as highly valuable by the driver.

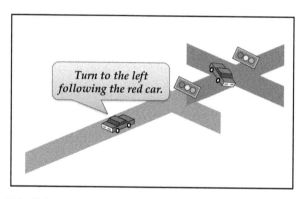

Figure 7.3. *Episode 1: information that specified the point of action by using an easy-to-understand reference for the driver (adapted from [KIT 09])*

7.4.3.2. *Episode 2*

Information which caused the driver to pay attention to events for safe driving (Figure 7.4) was considered helpful. The navigator told the driver that he/she should pay attention to motorcycles that would likely pass on the driver's side of the car. This area was near a university campus and many students had motorcycles.

7.4.3.3. *Episode 3*

Information helped the driver prepare for future actions, ensuring safe and smooth driving (Figure 7.5). When the driver was about to make a lane change from the current driver-side lane to the passenger-side lane in order to prepare for the next left turn, the navigator suggested remaining in the driver-side lane until the car had passed a mass home electronics retailer because it was likely that the passenger-side lane would be jammed with cars going to the retailer.

7.4.3.4. *Episode 4*

Information about interesting things seen along the route was helpful for driver. The navigator introduced the driver to a bakery where a variety of excellent breads were sold at reasonable prices. The navigator knew that the driver was interested in bread and that this information would be highly valuable for her/him.

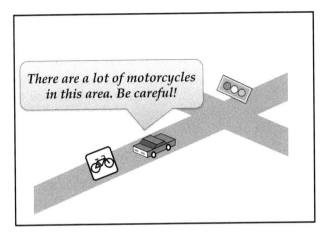

Figure 7.4. *Episode 2: information that caused the driver to pay attention to events for safe driving (adapted from [KIT 09])*

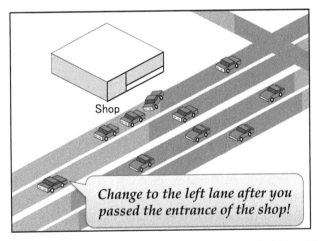

Figure 7.5. *Episode 3: information for safe and smooth driving. Note that cars drive on the left lanes in Japan (adapted from [KIT 09])*

7.5. Conclusions

This chapter illustrated a CCE study that identified three categories and 18 subcategories of information that drivers evaluated as necessary for safe and enjoyable driving. The mental processes for accomplishing train–station navigation tasks are slower than those for the tasks to follow the directions of a car navigation system (or a "human" car navigation system in this chapter), which is the example we illustrated at the beginning as shown in Figure I.2. The detailed workings of System 1 and System 2 would be different. However, since both share the time-critical features of interactions between human beings (passengers or drivers) and the environments, the case studies suggest that more suitable interactions design will be possible for those with specific cognitive characteristics for performing the tasks the interactions design should support satisfactorily. For example, for those suffering from information gathering tasks, or attention tasks, the critical indications, which are signboards in the case of train station and navigation directions in the case of car navigation systems, have to be placed where they expect to find them.

Information provided by a navigator is narrative in nature. Therefore, it should affect driver's System 2 before mode if it is given for the future driving behavior, or System 2 after mode if it is given for the past driving behavior. Whichever mode the navigator's information has influence on, the driver's memory should have been altered in combination with the associated processes carried out in System 1 before and/or after modes. The particular driving episodes associated with the navigator's information should have been processed consciously in System 2 before and/or after modes and therefore the memory trace created for the episode becomes consciously accessible when necessary in the future. We showed the role of conscious processing of an event while memorization for recalling it in the future consistent with the above-mentioned description through another CCE study where our participants were asked to watch short films at a theater [KIT 14b].

A practical implication found in this chapter is obtained by combining informational needs of drivers for safe and enjoyable driving as derived by the method described in this chapter with technological solutions that will make this happen. This information is very useful to consider how to design human–machine interface that should comfort to information processing processes of a driver as simulated by MHP/RT, which treats the cognitive functions that should work while driving, including working memory, attention, and planning that determine "how", and memory resonance that determines "what" as an integral unified autonomous system. For example, for a driver who does not know the area and is not good at merging and changing lanes, it would be useful for him/her to be given such instruction as "change to the left lane now because there is a merge from the right shortly". This is technologically feasible if there exists a system that can judge whether the following conditions are met:

1) the car is driving on the right lane;

2) there is a merge on the route;

3) it is possible to change to the left lane considering the current traffic condition;

4) the system can know the driver's attributes as described above.

In the past, little serious effort has been made on matching drivers' informational needs with technological considerations. The informational needs this chapter has identified, however, are not comprehensive. More studies will be necessary to investigate drivers' informational needs covering all driving situations.

8

Designing for Future Needs

This chapter describes how people's future needs are derived by applying CCE as discussed in Chapter 5. CCE assumes that people select their next behavior to maximize their satisfaction for given behavioral needs by appropriately coordinating available cognitive resources [KIT 13, KIT 12a]. CCE starts by defining critical parameters for understanding people's behavior by considering the nature of behavior selection processes in the field in question, and then designing ethnographical field observations. The participant's behavior is recorded, followed by a series of structured retrospective interviews. An analysis of the interview results aids in developing models of present behavior selections and their chronological changes in the past, which should trace the changes in people's behavioral needs and the structure of satisfaction. This chapter states that these models should serve as defining future needs of persons who would follow the same developing paths with a certain amount of time delay.

8.1. Introduction

The straightforward question for identifying people's *future needs* would be "what do you want in the near future?". However, it is inherently impossible for people to provide reliable answers to this question because they will not be able to accurately observe the state of the future world where their needs will be satisfied. Therefore, the concept *future needs* should be regarded as the concept inaccessible to those who are asked to express it at the present time. Since it is inherently impossible for a person to express his/her future needs reliably and accurately, a methodology for defining future needs should inevitably derive the person's future needs from outside of the person, e.g. from other individuals. This chapter illustrates how CCE has been successfully applied to derive future needs of people, drawing an example from spectators of professional baseball games. We suggest that the CCE-based methodology to derive future needs of people would be generally applicable to a variety of domains of human activities including IT devices equipped with HMI.

8.2. Making inaccessible future needs accessible: t-translation invariant principle

This section describes the idea of how to make inaccessible future needs accessible; in other words, how to define future needs of a person reliably and accurately that he/she cannot define as such by him/herself. A person has moment-by-moment desires for spending satisfactory and happy times in his/her living environment. Each person has his/her own unique living history. The personal history is stored in his/her long-term memory and significantly influences his/her way of reacting to his/her current environment with the given desire. What he/she wants to achieve at present can be considered as his/her present needs, $D(t = 0)$, and what he/she *will* consider at a certain time in the future, t, he/she wants to achieve given the present needs are satisfied,

$$D(t > 0) \text{ given } D(0) = \text{true} \quad \cdots \quad \text{a person's future needs}$$

can be considered as his/her future needs, which are not accessible at present. We want to know them without directly asking him/her what he/she thinks his/her future needs are.

Suppose a person, **A**, whose desire state at present, $t = 0$, is equal to the desire state of another person, **B**, in the past, $t = -\tau < 0$, i.e.

$$D_{\mathbf{A}}(t = 0 \text{ ; present}) = D_{\mathbf{B}}(t = -\tau \text{ ; past})$$

and this also applies to **A**'s history up to the past time,

$$t = -\sigma < 0$$

when **A** began to pay attention to the object toward which his/her desire is oriented now, and if the environment can be considered stable compared with the characteristic time of the change in the state of a person who interacts with this environment, it is likely that the person **A** will take the same developmental path as the person **B** has taken.

This situation is depicted by the following equation:

$$D_{\mathbf{A}}(t) = D_{\mathbf{B}}(t - \tau) \text{ for } -\sigma \le t \le \tau$$

In other words, **A** is behind **B** with the amount of time, τ, in terms of the change of desire state. In this scheme, defining future needs of **A** during the period spanning from the present, $t = 0$, to the future time, $t = \tau$, reduces to revealing the history of desire state of **B** from the past time, $t = -(\sigma + \tau)$, to the present, $t = 0$. It is suggested that this scheme should be called the "t-translation invariant principle" for making inaccessible future needs of a person accessible to those who want to understand and use the person's future needs at the present time. Figure 8.1 depicts it schematically.

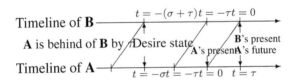

Figure 8.1. *t-Translation invariant principle*

The issue of predicting people's future needs has been dealt with in the field of ergonomics under the name of *prospective ergonomics*, which is about the conception and design of future systems, products or services [ROB 09]. However, as described, the problem of defining a person's future needs should be reduced to the problem of describing the other person's behavioral selection history, who is experiencing a certain amount of time ahead of the person in question; this is done by understanding a person's behavioral selection process in the past, which is, in large part, governed by memory processes, and therefore, it is the issue of the field of cognitive sciences.

The following sections describe a case study that illustrates the usefulness of CCE for extracting otherwise inaccessible people's future needs reliably and accurately.

8.3. A case study of CCE: why do fans repeat visits to the ballpark?

This section describes a case study of CCE. This study was started at the beginning of the 2008 regular season of Japan's professional baseball pennant race for the purpose of establishing a set of hypotheses concerning the processes of developing *repeaters* who regularly attend games hosted by the Hokkaido Nippon-Ham Fighters[1] at Sapporo Dome. Any person at the status of repeater must have reached at that status from lower statuses. The following sections describe in detail how the CCE study was conducted.

8.3.1. *Steps 1 and 2 of CCE*

The field of study was the ballpark of a Japanese professional baseball team, the Hokkaido Nippon-Ham Fighters. When the study was conducted, the Fighters had been there for 5 years. Those who had reached the status of repeater were expected to be able to reconstruct their histories to show how they had evolved from 2004 up until the time of the study. This study focused on the repeat visiting behavior of loyal fans of the Fighters. The specific study questions were: "Why do loyal fans repetitively visit Sapporo Dome to watch professional baseball games?" and "how have they evolved to their current status of loyal fans?".

As to how fans are structured, the following was concluded through a brief survey (Figure 8.2). Loyal fans, or repeaters, of a professional baseball team have their own individual histories in arriving at their current fan stage. They started in the pre-fan stage, passed through the fan stage and ultimately reached their current loyal-fan stage. In the pre-fan stage, fans know little

---

1 The Hokkaido Nippon-Ham Fighters is a professional baseball team in Japan's Pacific League. The team takes its name from the major shareholding company, Nippon Ham, which is the corporate name of Nippon Meat Packers Inc. In 2004, the Fighters moved from Tokyo to Sapporo, the largest city on the island of Hokkaido. The team uses Sapporo Dome, a stadium located in Toyohira-ku, Sapporo, Hokkaido, Japan, that is primarily used for football and baseball. Sapporo Dome opened in 2001 and currently has 42,126 seats. During the five years since the Fighters moved to Sapporo, its number of fans has increased dramatically. There were 38,776 fans registered with the official fan club in 2004, 41,817 in 2005, 41,193 in 2006, 60,216 in 2007 and 74,974 in 2008 (as of September 30th of each year). It is easy to enumerate plausible reasons behind the continuous increase in the number of fans. However, nobody knows exactly why the Fighters have achieved such great success.

about the team, or at most they pay a certain amount of attention to the team and/or have some interest in the team. However, their attitude toward the team is passive, and they exert no aggressive action. Starting from this pre-fan stage, they advance to the fan stage, when they aggressively desire to have a relationship with the team. For example, fan stage individuals display emotion toward the results of the games, and start to become interested in watching live games at the stadium. However, they do not have much interest in information about the team. A fan stage person advances to a loyal fan by breaking through these passive characteristics. Loyal stage fans aggressively collect information about the team, go to the stadium to watch live games when time allows or even arrange their activities so as to give top priority to watching live games at the stadium.

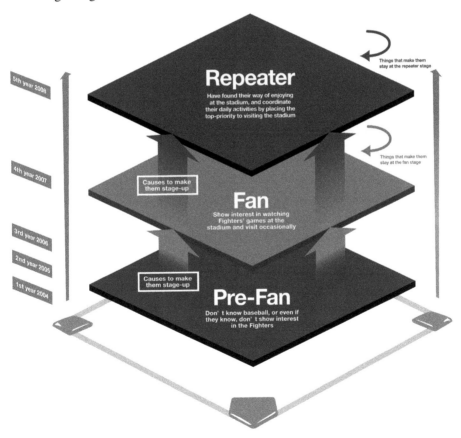

Figure 8.2. *Fan structure*

A number of aspects of MHP/RT's simulation of spectators are relevant to the CCE study at the ballpark. Referring to the Newell's time scale of human action [NEW 90], which is included in MHP/RT (Figure 2.11), the cognitive band with the characteristic times of ~100 msec to a few seconds is relevant to understand how a person reacts to the scene he/she is observing, i.e. real-time reactions to the live event. A "cheering" person would react to the events unconsciously but the other "analytic" person would analyze scene by scene as if he were the coach of the team. The former would construct memory different from the one the latter would create. These differences might result in different courses of development toward the loyal-fan stage. In fact, Kitajima et al. [KIT 11b] found that their participants at a movie theater had created two essentially different memories of the same event on the screen depending on the degree of participation of consciousness while encoding events.

On the other hand, the rational band with the characteristic times of ~10 minutes to hours is relevant to understand how a person would expect or reflect on a specific game or specific segments within a game. Some persons would engage in these activities intentionally but the others would not. This aspect might be considered in the "cheering versus analytic" dimension as well.

Finally, the social band with the characteristic times of approximately weeks to months is relevant to reflecting on the past seasons and deciding how to behave for the coming season, i.e. pennant race, or participate in the events during the off-season. It was assumed that the number of cycles of on-season and off-season would affect the overall attitude of how to enjoy visiting ball park.

In this way, two critical parameters were derived for the study: one was the viewing attitude parameter and the other was the length of fan history parameter. In addition, the latter two bands, rational and social, are also related with the purposes of visiting and enjoying ball games at the stadium; a variety of purposes, or goals, are listed in MSA [KIT 07], a subtheory of MHP/RT. One may enjoy him/herself, one may want to have his/her family members enjoy, one may want to purchase a special premium goods, etc. These aspects would be considered in the interview step, step 5.

8.3.2. *Step 3 of CCE: monitor recruiting*

We conducted a Web survey for 3 consecutive days (11 June, 2008 to 13 June, 2008) and selected nine highly loyal fans, i.e. elite monitors, from the Fighters' fan club members who had different attitudes toward professional baseball, and had visited Sapporo Dome several times since the Fighters moved to Sapporo in 2004. The number of responses was 3,687. The selection process consisted of two stages. The first stage was to select 30 respondents as candidates for the elite monitors. We conducted a series of group interview sessions with six candidates as one group for the purpose of confirming their responses to the Web survey and, most importantly, their attitudes toward the study: we wanted elite monitors who had little problem in expressing their own fan history and their behavior at the stadium, i.e. talkative and cooperative. We finally selected nine elite monitors. The nine selected fans were supposed to represent different "fan styles" and had different histories in reaching their current fan status as defined by the hypothesis as described. The number "nine" came from several constraints for conducting the study, i.e. the amount of budget, the schedule of the games at the stadium, the location and the number of seats reserved for the study, the number of equipment for recording, etc.

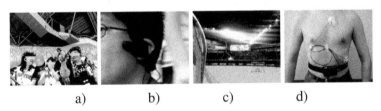

a)   b)   c)   d)

Figure 8.3. *Illustration of the field observation: a) three elite monitors in their seats watching a game, b) ear-mounted CCD camera, c) the view of the ear-mount camera and d) an electrocardiograph and an accelerometer*

8.3.3. *Step 4 of CCE: field observation*

We had the elite monitors visit Sapporo Dome three times to watch designated Fighters-hosted games. We recorded their viewing behavior using a DVD camera recorder located three rows in front of the monitors' seats to capture their game-viewing behavior (Figure 8.3(a)), installing a small ear-mounted   CCD   camera   to   record   the   scene   they   were viewing (Figures 8.3(b) and (c)), recording their vocalizations with a pin microphone and using an electrocardiograph and an accelerometer to capture their physiological responses to the events of the game (Figure 8.3(d)). The designated games were a three-game series with the Softbank Hawks in July, a three-game series with the Orix Buffalos in August and a three-game series with the Rakuten Golden Eagles in September. Each elite monitor was asked to attend all three series.

Figure 8.4. *A screen shot from the interview session*

8.3.4. *Step 5 of CCE: conduct retrospective interviews*

We conducted structured interviews after each visit to Sapporo Dome, replaying the behavior recordings, the viewing scene recordings and the broadcasted TV video of the game for the characteristic events, including scoring scenes, field events between innings and events for which the participants exhibited remarkable changes in physiological data (Figure 8.4). Each participant was interviewed three times.

Each interview lasted 90 minutes, and therefore each elite monitor was interviewed for 270 minutes in total. The purpose of the first interview was to understand how the participants enjoyed the game. The purpose of the second interview was to understand how participants developed their loyalty from the pre-fan stage several years ago, to the fan stage a few years ago and then to the current repeaters stage. The purpose of the third interview was to understand what triggered the state changes and what factors helped them retain each fan stage. The interviewers required to keep the workings of MHP/RT, e.g. a large part of behavioral selections is unconscious and therefore hard to tell intellectual "reasons" for them, in mind not only while conducting the interview sessions but also when analyzing the collected data.

8.3.5. *Step 6 of CCE: socioecological model construction*

We compiled the results of the interviews in the form of a fan loyalty evolution diagram (FLE diagram) that represented in detail how individual participants had evolved their loyalty by specifying triggers for stage changes, circumstances that made them stay at a particular stage and activities in both the regular season and in the off-season (Figure 8.5 and Table 8.1). Nine FLE diagrams were created. We then compiled them to derive models of developmental processes of repeaters, which will be described in the following section.

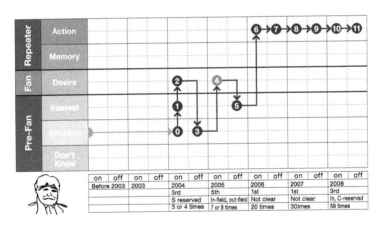

Figure 8.5. *A participant's fan history during the period from 2004 to 2008*

8.3.5.1. *Results: developmental processes of repeaters*

The following section describes results of analysis of the evidence collected during the interview sessions that focused on triggers that caused monitors to step up a stage (i.e. from pre-fan stage to fan stage, and from fan stage to loyal-fan stage), and the conditions that made or make them stay in a particular stage. These triggers and conditions define a rough qualitative model of the developmental process of fan loyalty along the time dimension.

Number	Year	On/Off	Event
0	2004	On	Not interested in baseball. Not interested in the Fighters coming to Sapporo.
1	2004	On	Obtained information about the team and the players in relation to his job as journalist.
2	2004	On	Had come to pay attention to some players.
3	2004	Off	Knew about the players' trade, salary, etc.
4	2005	On	Joined the official fan club and net communities. Watched TV.
5	2005	Off	Got access to the information during season off, but not actively.
6	2006	On	Cheered with a player's T-shirt. Began to repeat at the end of the season.
7	2006	Off	Participated in the parade for championship, events and talk shows.
8	2007	On	Went to the Sapporo Dome stadium after work when possible. Cheered with replica uniform.
9	2007	Off	Participated in the events. Purchased the passport ticket.
10	2008	On	Visited the farm and visitor games. Began to purchase goods. Started to limit the amount of purchases.
11	2008	Off	Got access to the information during the season off, but not actively.

Table 8.1. *The events that happened in respective years that characterize the fan level of events*

8.3.5.1.1. Progressing from the pre-fan stage to the fan stage

Three common triggers were found in the study for advancing the elite monitors from the pre-fan stage to the fan stage.

1) "Retirement of a star player" and "expectation of league championship": In the 2006 regular season, two events triggered three participants who had little knowledge about professional baseball, and another three participants who had knowledge about professional baseball but did not have enough interest in it, to progress to the fan stage. One event was an announcement by the then star player, outfielder Tsuyoshi Shinjo, that he was retiring, relatively early in the regular season. This news was reported frequently in various media. The other event was that the Fighters were in the first championship race of the league and Japan's professional baseball leagues.

2) "Watch the fans cheering": Two participants who had little knowledge about professional baseball and one participant who had little interest in

professional baseball advanced to the fan stage after watching live cheering in the stadium.

3) "Know the players and the team" and "unexpected talent of players outside baseball": Regardless of their knowledge level of professional baseball, knowing players and the team triggered participants to progress to the fan stage. Three participants who knew professional baseball reacted to the players' behavior outside baseball, causing them to advance to the fan stage.

8.3.5.1.2. Advancing from the fan stage to the loyal-fan stage

Ten common triggers were found in the study for advancing the elite monitors from the fan stage to the loyal-fan stage:

1) "Watching live games at the stadium".

2) "Knowing the rules of baseball and the team".

3) "Watching games by oneself", "one's wife became a fan by following his lead", "communication with his/her friends at the stadium" or "meeting persons who visited the stadium": The common feature of these triggers is the establishment of an environment where fans could comfortably watch the games at the stadium with someone who contributed to building a relationship with them (e.g. spouse or friends).

4) "Presence of players who always come to mind": Participants who had little knowledge about baseball or professional baseball, those who were fans of other professional baseball teams, and those who became fans at the end of the regular seasons tended to find opportunities that should provide information about players, teams and the Fighters in particular. These participants were eager to attend off-season events such as talk shows and advanced to loyal fans in the next regular season.

5) "Collecting the Fighters' merchandise".

6) "Recording events of live games" and/or "collecting the recordings as proof of watching the games".

7) "Expectation of the climax series and the Nippon series", and "eagerness to watch those series".

8) "Communication with the other fans when watching live games".

9) "Network community" that they accessed during live games to exchange information and post opinions.

10) "Seeing the players closely, e.g. visiting camp in Okinawa", and those who had special interest (or who followed pro-baseball) said that their greatest interest was in seeing live action on a professional field.

8.3.6. *Results: developing from a pre-fan to a repeater*

While they were in the pre-fan stage, the nine elite monitors were classified into three categories in terms of their interest in baseball or professional baseball:

1) three elite monitors did not have any interest in baseball;

2) another three were interested in baseball in general but did not have interest in professional baseball;

3) the rest had interest in professional baseball but were not interested in purchasing tickets to visit Sapporo Dome for watching Fighters' games.

Figure 8.6 illustrates the cases of the Group A and Group C. The pre-fans who did not know baseball well, Group A, have developed into either repeaters who enjoy cheering or those who enjoy watching games (Figure 8.6, top). The pre-fans in the Group C category have developed into repeaters who enjoy watching games (Figure 8.6, bottom).

8.3.6.1. *Defining future needs by CCE*

This section starts by discussing how the t-translation invariant principle could be applied for the fans of the professional baseball team. In this study, the trajectories of the elite monitors from 2004 to 2008 could be considered as typical developmental paths from their pre-fan stage, to their fan stage and ultimately to their loyal-fan stage. The common triggers were identified for developing from the pre-fan stage to the fan stage, and from the fan stage to the loyal-fan stage (see [KIT10] for more details). The principle claims for a fan's future needs as follows, if we go back to the year of 2008, for example:

A fan at his/her pre-fan stage now, i.e. the year of 2008, whose attitude toward the professional baseball team is the same as one of the elite monitor's, say **E**, will take the same developmental path from 2008 to 2012 as **E** has taken from 2004 to 2008 given the appropriate triggers are to be provided to him/her timely.

As shown in Figure 8.6, the developmental paths of the nine elite monitors depended on their attitude toward the professional baseball team when they had been in the pre-fan stage. This suggests that questionnaires concerning their attitudes toward professional baseball, e.g. "do you have knowledge about baseball?", "do you know about professional baseball?", "do you purchase tickets for watching professional baseball game at the stadium", would be useful to classify a fan into the fan similar to those shown in Figure 8.6. Effective triggers may be different, as discussed in section 8.3.5.1.

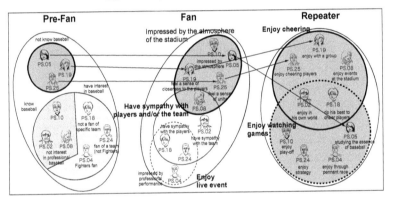

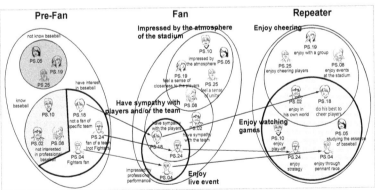

Figure 8.6. *The evolution trajectory of each elite monitor. Left: the paths for those who had not known baseball when they were at the pre-fan stage. Right: the paths for those who had not been fan of this specific team when they were at the pre-fan stage*

8.4. Discussion

8.4.1. *Selection of elite monitors*

In this case study, nine elite monitors were selected from 3,687 respondents of the Web survey. The selection process of elite monitors is similar to purposeful sampling that is normally used in qualitative studies. Purposeful sampling is significantly different from random sampling in which the purpose of the study is to understand average characteristics of the population from which the samples are selected randomly.

CCE is interested in the study question "what would such and such people do in such and such a way in such and such a circumstance?". It is not "what would average people do in such and such a circumstance?". CCE is also interested in understanding people's behavior along the time dimension. Therefore, CCE naturally involves the processes of recording monitors' behavior in the real field and retrospective interview sessions for identifying monitors' memory that should have been active when the behavior was recorded. From these data, the investigators try to reconstruct the elite monitors' individual histories with a focus on the critical parameters. The histories thus created could be compared within the parameter space defined by the critical parameters to derive useful insights that should provide deeper understanding of the people, among whom the elite monitors should be appropriately located. In this way, elite monitors are the precious resource for the study and needed to be selected carefully.

8.4.2. *CCE interview*

The main purpose of a CCE study is to reconstruct the participant's behavioral trajectory in order to answer the question "what would such and such people do in such and such a way in such and such a circumstance?". What we observed in the study field is used in the interview sessions in which the investigators and the participant would engage in the project of reconstructing the participant's history relevant to the purpose of the study. Figure 8.5 and Table 8.1 illustrate the typical results of the interview sessions.

What the investigators should extract in the interview sessions are the descriptions of the contents of long-term memory that are related with the contents that are active in the participant's working memory, which originally come from the recorded data shown to the participant serving as the cues to make available the contents in long-term memory. Figure 8.4 illustrates such an interview session. The image displayed on the screen would be used to create some representations in working memory which would then serve as the initial cues for activating relevant portions of long-term memory.

In general, investigators tend to search for causal relations among events; when an event comes after another one, they are inclined to understand the event sequence in such a way that "the latter should have caused the former, and therefore there should be a reason why the participant did that way as evidenced by the event, observed or described". However, as Two Minds processing strongly suggests [KAH 03], people often make intuitive decisions that inevitably would lead to unconscious behavior, which should not be associated with any rational reasons. On the other hand, the participants tend to provide "intellectual" answers when they are asked "why did you do that way?" because they want to be evaluated as a rational being. What the investigators would obtain are spurious reasons that may lead to the wrong understandings of the participants behavioral trajectories. We suggest that reconstruction of the participants' behavioral trajectories should be carried out with the focus of how the contents of long-term memory should have evolved considering the memory processes of MHP/RT [KIT 13].

8.4.3. *Applicability of CCE*

The interview step is key for the reconstruction process. However, the format of interview, namely, the investigators typically ask question verbally and the participants give answers verbally, or via symbols with the shared meaning, should place restrictions on the range of the reconstruction. This is again related with the memory process. As shown in Chapter 3, each system has its own memory, i.e. RMD frame for the conscious process and BMD frame for the unconscious process, and both may be integrated to construct a memory that is accessible from the conscious process and/or the unconscious process.

However, there are cases where a BMD frame is not integrated with a RMD frame, which was actually evidenced in the study concerning how people enjoy watching short films [KIT 11b]. Since the interview uses symbols as the representations for getting access to long-term memory of the participants and for having the participants describe the contents of long-term memory, the pieces of memory that are not integrated with the RMD frame are not accessible via symbolic representations. For example, when a participant is shown a scene that he/she has actually watched and to which he/she showed strong physiological reactions, and he/she is asked to report the consequence of a scene; if he/she has only the memory of the scene in the BMD frame, he/she will not be able to associate the memory with any reportable symbols. He/she will be able to activate certain memory traces in the BMD frame that is associated with the scene, but they are not labeled as "the consequence of the scene" because this requires integration with the RMD frame. Therefore, he/she will not be able to provide any useful answers to construct his behavioral trajectories. As mentioned in section 2.5.2.1, he/she is working in MHP/RT Mode 3 or MHP/RT Mode 4 in which the conscious process of System 2 and the unconscious process of System 1 work asynchronously, and therefore integration of the RMD frame and the BMD frame has not happened. In other words, CCE is applicable for those who work in MHP/RT Mode 1 or MHP/RT Mode 2 in which the conscious process and the unconscious process work in parallel and memory will be constructed by integrating RMD frame and BMD frame.

8.5. Conclusions

This chapter began with the claim that people would never be able to imagine their future accurately and reliably, nor what they would need in an unknown future. However, there are needs in a variety of fields for knowing people's future needs. This chapter proposed a solution by introducing the idea of people's behavioral trajectories – some of which may advance a certain amount of time from the others – and the principled way of reconstructing people's behavioral trajectories, CCE, whose basis is provided by the cognitive architecture, MHP/RT, that is capable of simulating people's decision-making or action selection processes in daily life.

Understanding people's decision-making in daily activities is crucial for CCE studies. There are two forms of understanding: quantitative understanding and qualitative understanding. Quantitative understanding is derived through statistical data analyses applied to a large collection of data, implicitly assuming that noise in the collected data should obey some form of probabilistic distribution. This form of understanding involves identifying causal relationships among entities in the data. Rational interpretations of the data are expected. This might be possible if the data were generated solely by the rational processing system. In contrast, qualitative understanding is derived through studies in natural settings that try to uncover the regularities in the behavioral trajectories, such as common triggers for promoting them to higher fan stages.

Considering the nature of decision-making and action selection at the site in question, the observed behavior should in a large part be the result of immediate actions controlled by the experiential processing system. Such decision-making and action selection may not be rational, but is controlled by the bounded rationality principle and the satisficing principle uncovered by Simon [SIM 56] and further studied by Kahneman [KAH 03] in generating situated decision-making and action selection. As Newell [NEW 90] suggested, the conscious processes and the unconscious processes occur in the different bands with different characteristic times. It is not wise to try to understand the phenomena in the higher bands by extrapolating the findings in the lower bands, i.e. to try to understand rational behaviors by treating unconscious behaviors as subsidiaries as ACT-R [AND 98, AND 07]. This book has advanced the line established by Simon [SIM 56] and Kahneman [KAH 03] even further by introducing the cognitive architecture, MHP/RT, for simulating people's daily decision-making and action selection, whose differences are discussed in Kitajima and Toyota [KIT 13], and the methodology, CCE, for conducting field study to understand people's decision-making and action selection process, of which prescription is given by MHP/RT.

This chapter illustrated a case study that applied the CCE methodology for reconstructing history of fans of a professional baseball team. The unique feature is the selection of monitors, called elite monitors, who should represent respective segments defined by combinations of values of critical parameters that should be effective to distinguish among the behaviors of fans. There are those fans who are a certain amount of time, say 2 years, behind an elite monitor and would follow the same behavioral trajectory as the elite monitor. However, we need a method to find those fans, which should be challenged in the future.

The case study revealed histories of nine elite monitors, which demonstrated how they moved through the fan stages, from the pre-fan stage to the fan stage and ultimately to the loyal-fan stage. We identified features that motivated participants to advance from the fan stage, and those that motivated them to advance from the fan stage to the loyal-fan stage. These features should suggest possible paths that potential loyal fans follow and define possible their needs when they are at the pre-fan stage and those when they are at the fan stage in the future.

Conclusion

Technique versus Skill Viewed from MHP/RT's Four-Processes

As the final section of this book, this Conclusion tries to consider the relationships between HMI and MHP/RT from a wider perspective by integrating what has been described in the previous chapters. MHP/RT shows that the processes of action selection and memorization are cyclic and are carried out in the four distinct processing modes. How they actually work has been described in Chapters 6 and 7. The cyclic process has continued for years driven by behavioral needs defined by the satisfaction structure of human beings. Chapter 8 (section 8.3) discussed how changes in behavioral needs occur in overt behavior. The trace of moment-by-moment interaction with the environment accumulates in human memory and affects action selection processes. This chapter considers how it can be viewed based on what has been explained so far in this book and derives implication to HMI design.

Two distinct forms of HMI in using artifacts: technique and skill[1]

MHP/RT describes people's daily behavior as a cyclic process of action selection and memory formation. In our daily life, we spend a lot of time in interacting with artifacts, and therefore it is obvious that it should affect development of individual memory systems. At the same time, any particular artifacts that exist as they are should embed in themselves their own histories including their predecessors. Occasional innovations might have caused evolution of memory structure of mankind through people's interaction with the artifacts through HMI, and might have resulted in "splicing" evolution in the sociocultural ecology. MHP/RT suggests that the cyclic processes should

---

1 The description of this section is from [KIT 15a].

define strong constraints on sustainable innovation; as far as the cyclic processes function in utilizing an artifact implemented in a technological innovation, it should survive, otherwise it should disappear. This chapter contrasts technique and skill, the two distinct forms of HMI in using artifacts, and derives guidelines for designing sustainable HMI that should support smooth development of people's skill necessary for using artifacts from their mere use through the technique.

	Technique	Skill
Human behavior	planned ways of doing something, or, methods	body movements
Objects (Artifacts)	machines	tools; combination of available tools
Acquisition procedure	learning algorithm, principles and theories	mimicking teacher's behavior
What is acquired	multidimensional parametric solutions, could be generalized and automatized	analog solutions for a given boundary condition defined by the musculo-skeletal system and the external environment
Adaptation to the external environment	pay attention to a limited range of perceptual stimuli; strengthening and increasing accuracy in accordance with the evolution of technique	flexible and adaptive; in mimicking, a learner takes information from a teacher visually and selects appropriate body movements from the learned ones, and coordinates them
Development	stepwise	trail and error; incremental; body movement practice
Propagation	mediated by language; easily spread broadly and accumulated over time	mediated by mimicking, language not effective; spreading speed is limited
Examples	computers; general purpose machines; autonomous adaptive machines	tools; single-purpose machines; machine dolls

Table 1. *Characteristics of technique and skill*

Technique

Technique is a special way of doing something, or method, which is a planned way of doing something with the artifact, especially artifact that a lot of people know about and use. In other words, there are some principles or theories, both are normally explicitly expressed in language concerning what is the artifact and how it should work. The artifact is defined in a multidimensional parametric space and therefore its use by people can be generalized and automatized by some algorithm. Form the four processes point of view, technique is more related with System 2 before/after mode, and likely to be stored in declarative memory.

Since an artifact is defined in a parametric space, a person needs to pay attention to a limited range of perceptual stimuli. A person can deal with some fluctuations in the behavior of the artifact if he/she has or infer some motor algorithm that is linked with the perceptual representation of the input. By definition, technique is specific to some aspect of doing something. Because of this, the more a technique develops over time, the more robust and accurate it becomes. An advanced technique is expressed as a very detailed plan for doing something, which enables a person to do something with increased strength and accuracy. As such, technique is amenable to language. Any technique can be learned systematically where grammatically and pragmatically adequate language would be used to create written materials for facilitating learning. Evolution of technique should be stepwise and discrete. Technique is easily spread among people and accumulates over time. Technique can be considered as something like a memory that includes its associated developing history [STI 08]. Table 1 summarizes the features of technique. Examples shown in the table are expected to work properly within some predefined range of the work situations.

Skill

On the other hand, skill refers to an ability to do something well, especially because you have learned and practiced it. From the four processes point of view, skill is likely to be stored in procedural memory. Skill is more related with body movement than knowing something, required for technique, in relation with some artifacts operated through associated body movements. Skill is acquired via repetitive practices by mainly observing the way how teachers use the artifact and mimicking by moving their body parts as they observe them. As for the results, skill in a larger scale can be viewed as the results of combining necessary mimicked body movements constrained by the musculoskeletal system. Body movements are realized under the strong constraints of the musculoskeletal system, and therefore the actually observed well-practiced body movements for a specific boundary condition should be optimal in terms of energy consumption governed by kinematics: this derives analog solutions for a given boundary condition defined by the musculoskeletal system and the external environment. Therefore, actual manifestation of skill should be regarded as an analog one-dimensional solution for the situation in question.

Skill acquisition is flexible and adaptive. Through mimicking, a learner takes information from a teacher visually and selects appropriate body movements adaptively. Then, individual movements are coordinated with each other. However, the parts of the body where the body movements are executed are constructed from cells and therefore there are limitations in strength and accuracy. Reflecting on these inherent features, skill is acquired gradually through trail and error practices that should train the links between the sensory system with motor system. Any skill is learned through mimicking. This means that language is not an appropriate medium. Skill acquisition by mimicking is possible when overt behavior, or body movement, is linked with covert neural activities that cause the motor movements. As such, the kinds of object that skill acquisition should occur include tools, single purpose machines, mechanical dolls and so on.

Conditions for sustainable and evolving HMI

Whatever artifacts that exist at the moment could be objects for technique and/or skill. They exist as they are in the current sociocultural ecology, which in turn is defined by how the artifacts function there, and both, artifacts and sociocultural ecology, evolve over time as interacting with each other. Therefore, the shape of ecology could become very diverse. As shown in the previous section, technique and skill have important differences. But technique could turn into skill if conditions are satisfied and the skill could be incorporated into a new technique. When this spiral evolution occurs, the sociocultural ecology where the artifacts are embedded will evolve, to show splicing evolution.

When a new goal is set, it is necessary for the ecology to generate a new path to accomplish the goal, which is carried out by means of splicing. The process is splicing because there are two distinct approaches in it and they must be integrated into a unity as a new path: one approach includes unconscious bodily operations and the other includes consciousness operations. The former is more fundamental to human activities practiced by a lot of people for a long time: the approach includes improving bodily movements and/or tools. The latter approach has been established by modern cultures. It requires improvement of language from superficial, phenomenological approach to structural, logical approach. Only after this improvement has been accomplished can the ecology apply this approach for accomplishing a new goal. In this approach, we use structural language consciously to analyze the paths for accomplishing exiting goals and generate a hypothetical path for accomplishing the new goal based on the analysis of existing paths. We can imagine a new path by applying structural analysis concerning how to achieve the new goal in the given environment, which is called innovation. For the segments included along the path that cannot be accomplished by unconscious bodily movements, improvement of bodily movements and/or tools will be required, or new artifacts will be designed for otherwise impossible movements. In this way, since the new path for the new goal is defined structurally by conscious language and operationally by bodily movements, it looks like a splicing development.

As the MHP/RT's four processes shows, there are cases where technique and skill are mutually related with each other via a common event through a *perceptual* multidimensional frame [KIT 14c]. However, there are cases where the technique is defined in such a way that it does not link well with the acquired existing skills that should work when the event is just about to come without any deep considerations. In these cases, there will be no splicing evolution expected. This is an important caveat in designing artifacts.

Bibliography

[AND 93] ANDERSON J.R., *Rules of the Mind*, Lawrence Erlbaum Associates, Hillsdale, NJ, 1993.

[AND 98] ANDERSON J.R., LEBIERE C., *The Atomic Components of Thought*, Lawrence Erlbaum Associates, Mahwah, NJ, 1998.

[AND 07] ANDERSON J.R., *How Can the Human Mind Occur in the Physical Universe?*, Oxford University Press, New York, NY, 2007.

[DAM 99] DAMASIO A., *Feeling of What Happens: Body and Emotion in the Making of Consciousness*, Houghton Mifflin Harcourt, Orlando, FL, 1999.

[DAW 76] DAWKINS R., *The Selfish Gene*, Oxford University Press, New York, NY, 1976.

[EVA 09] EVANS J.S.B.T., FRANKISH K., (eds.), *In Two Minds: Dual Processes and Beyond*, Oxford University Press, Oxford, 2009.

[FU 07] FU W.-T., PIROLLI P., "SNIF-ACT: a cognitive model of user navigation on the World Wide Web", *Human-Machine Interaction*, vol. 22, no. 4, pp. 355–412, 2007.

[KAH 03] KAHNEMAN D., "A perspective on judgment and choice", *American Psychologist*, vol. 58, no. 9, pp. 697–720, 2003.

[KAH 11] KAHNEMAN D., *Thinking, Fast and Slow*, Farrar, Straus and Giroux, New York, NY, 2011.

[KIN 88] KINTSCH W., "The use of knowledge in discourse processing: a construction-integration model", *Psychological Review*, vol. 95, pp. 163–182, 1988.

[KIN 98] KINTSCH W., *Comprehension: A Paradigm for Cognition*, Cambridge University Press, Cambridge, UK, 1998.

[KIT 00] KITAJIMA M., BLACKMON M.H., POLSON P.G., "A Comprehension-based model of web navigation and its application to web usability analysis", in MCDONALD S., WAERN Y., COCKTON G., (eds.), *People and Computers XIV: Usability or Else! (Proceedings of HCI 2000)*, London, Springer, pp. 357–373, 2000.

[KIT 07] Kitajima M., Shimada H., Toyota M., "MSA:maximum satisfaction architecture—a basis for designing intelligent autonomous agents on WEB 2.0", in McNamara D.S., Trafton J.G., (eds)., *Proceedings of the 29th Annual Conference of the Cognitive Science Society*, Cognitive Science Society, Austin, TX, p. 1790, 2007.

[KIT 08] Kitajima M., Toyota M., Shimada H., "The model brain: brain information hydrodynamics (BIH)in", Love B.C., McRae K., Sloutsky V.M., (eds)., *Proceedings of the 30th Annual Conference of the Cognitive Science Society*, Cognitive Science Society, Austin, TX, p. 1453, 2008.

[KIT 09] Kitajima M., Akamatsu M., Maruyama Y. et al., "Information for helping drivers achieve safe and enjoyable driving: an on-road observational study", *Proceedings of the Human Factors and Ergonomics Society 53rd Annual Meeting 2009*, Human Factors and Ergonomics Society, Santa Monica, CA, pp. 1801–1805, 2009.

[KIT10] Kitajima M., Nakajima M., Toyota M., "Cognitive chrono-ethnography: a method for studying behavioral selections in daily activities", *Proceedings of the Human Factors and Ergonomics Society 54th Annual Meeting*, Human Factors and Ergonomics Society, Santa Monica, CA, pp. 1732–1736, 2010.

[KIT 11a] Kitajima M., Toyota M., "Four processing modes of *in situ* human behavior", in Samsonovich A.V., Jóhannsdóttir K.R. (eds.), *Biologically Inspired Cognitive Architectures 2011: Proceedings of the Second Annual Meeting of the BICA Society*, IOS Press, Amsterdam, The Netherlands, pp. 194–199, 2011.

[KIT 11b] Kitajima M., Toyota M., Yoshino K. et al., "Relationship between episodic memory formation and two minds", *Proceedings of the 33rd Annual Conference of the Cognitive Science Society*, Cognitive Science Society, Boston, USA, p. 2095, 2011.

[KIT 12a] Kitajima M., Toyota M., "Simulating navigation behaviour based on the architecture model model human processor with real-time constraints (MHP/RT)", *Behaviour & Information Technology*, vol. 31, no. 1, pp. 41–58, 2012.

[KIT 12b] Kitajima M., Toyota M., "The role of memory in MHP/RT: organization, function and operation", *Proceedings of ICCM 2012: 11th International Conference on Cognitive Modeling*, Berlin, Germany, pp. 291–296, 2012.

[KIT 13] Kitajima M., Toyota M., "Decision-making and action selection in Two Minds: an analysis based on model human processor with realtime constraints (MHP/RT)", *Biologically Inspired Cognitive Architectures*, vol. 5, pp. 82–93, 2013.

[KIT 14a] Kitajima M., Toyota M., "Hierarchical structure of human action selections: an update of Newell's time scale of human action", *Procedia Computer Science, BICA 2014. 5th Annual International Conference on Biologically Inspired Cognitive Architectures*, vol. 99, pp. 321–325, 2014.

[KIT 14b] Kitajima M., Toyota M., "The role of consciousness in memorization: asymmetric functioning of consciousness in memory encoding and decoding", *Procedia Computer Science, BICA 2014. 5th Annual International Conference on Biologically Inspired Cognitive Architectures*, vol. 99, pp. 309–320, 2014.

[KIT 14c] KITAJIMA M., TOYOTA M., "Topological considerations of memory structure", *Procedia Computer Science, BICA 2014. 5th Annual International Conference on Biologically Inspired Cognitive Architectures*, vol. 99, pp. 326–331, 2014.

[KIT 15a] KITAJIMA M., TOYOTA M., "Guidelines for designing artifacts for the dual-process", *Procedia Computer Science, BICA 2015. 6th Annual International Conference on Biologically Inspired Cognitive Architectures*, Lyon, France, 6–8 November 2015.

[KIT 15b] KITAJIMA M., TOYOTA M., "Two minds and emotion", *COGNITIVE 2015: The Seventh International Conference on Advanced Cognitive Technologies and Applications*, Nice, France, pp. 8–16, 2015.

[MCC 87] MCCLELLAND J.L., RUMELHART D.E., GROUP P.R., *Parallel Distributed Processing: Explorations in the Microstructure of Cognition: Psychological and Biological Models (A Bradford Book)*, The MIT Press, Cambrige MA, vol. 7, 1987.

[MOR 06] MORRIS D., *The Nature of Happiness*, Little Books Ltd., London, 2006.

[NEW 90] NEWELL A., *Unified Theories of Cognition (The William James Lectures, 1987)*, Harvard University Press, Cambridge, MA, 1990.

[OLS 03] OLSTON C., CHI E.H., "ScentTrails: integrating browsing and searching on the Web", *ACM Transactions on Computer-Human Interaction*, vol. 10, no. 3, pp. 177–197, 2003.

[PAY 91] PAYNE S.J., "Display-based action at the user interface", *International Journal of Man-Machine Studies*, vol. 35, no. 3, pp. 275–289, 1991.

[PRI 85] PRIGOGINE I., STENGERS I., *Order Out of Chaos: Man's New Dialogue with Nature*, Fontana Press, Waukegan, Illinois, 1985.

[ROB 09] ROBERT J.-M., BRANGIER E., "What Is prospective ergonomics? A reflection and a position on the future of ergonomics", *Proceedings of the International Conference on Ergonomics and Health Aspects of Work with Computers: Held As Part of HCI International 2009*, EHAWC '09, Springer-Verlag, Berlin, Heidelberg, pp. 162–169, 2009.

[SIM 56] SIMON H.A., "Rational choice and the structure of the environment", *Psychological Review*, vol. 63, pp. 129–138, 1956.

[STI 08] STIEGLER B., *Technics and Time, 2: Disorientation (Meridian: Crossing Aesthetics)*, Stanford University Press, Redwood City, California, vol. 10, 2008.

[SUT 10] SUTO S., KUMADA T., "Effects of age-related decline of visual attention, working memory and planning functions on use of IT-equipment", *Japanese Psychological Research*, vol. 52, pp. 201–215, 2010.

[SWA 11] SWANSON L.W., *Brain Architecture*, Oxford University Press, Great Clarendon Street, Oxford, UK, 2011.

[TOY 08] TOYOTA M., KITAJIMA M., SHIMADA H., "Structured meme theory: how is informational inheritance maintained?", in LOVE B.C., MCRAE K., SLOUTSKY V.M., (eds.), *Proceedings of the 30th Annual Conference of the Cognitive Science Society*, Cognitive Science Society, Austin, TX, p. 2288, 2008.

Index

Other titles from

in

Information Systems, Web and Pervasive Computing

2015

ARDUIN Pierre-Emmanuel, GRUNDSTEIN Michel,
ROSENTHAL-SABROUX Camille
Information and Knowledge System

BÉRANGER Jérôme
Medical Information Systems Ethics

BRONNER Gérald
Belief and Misbelief Asymmetry on the Internet

IAFRATE Fernando
From Big Data to Smart Data

KRICHEN Saoussen, BEN JOUIDA Sihem
Supply Chain Management and its Applications in Computer Science

NEGRE Elsa
Information and Recommender Systems

POMEROL Jean-Charles, EPELBOIN Yves, THOURY Claire
MOOCs

2012

BUCHER Bénédicte, LE BER Florence
Innovative Software Development in GIS

GAUSSIER Eric, YVON François
Textual Information Access

STOCKINGER Peter
Audiovisual Archives: Digital Text and Discourse Analysis

VENTRE Daniel
Cyber Conflict

2011

BANOS Arnaud, THÉVENIN Thomas
Geographical Information and Urban Transport Systems

DAUPHINÉ André
Fractal Geography

LEMBERGER Pirmin, MOREL Mederic
Managing Complexity of Information Systems

STOCKINGER Peter
Introduction to Audiovisual Archives

STOCKINGER Peter
Digital Audiovisual Archives

VENTRE Daniel
Cyberwar and Information Warfare

2010

BONNET Pierre
Enterprise Data Governance

BRUNET Roger
Sustainable Geography

CARREGA Pierre
Geographical Information and Climatology

CAUVIN Colette, ESCOBAR Francisco, SERRADJ Aziz
Thematic Cartography – 3-volume series
Thematic Cartography and Transformations – volume 1
Cartography and the Impact of the Quantitative Revolution – volume 2
New Approaches in Thematic Cartography – volume 3

LANGLOIS Patrice
Simulation of Complex Systems in GIS

MATHIS Philippe
Graphs and Networks – 2nd edition

THERIAULT Marius, DES ROSIERS François
Modeling Urban Dynamics

2009

BONNET Pierre, DETAVERNIER Jean-Michel, VAUQUIER Dominique
Sustainable IT Architecture: the Progressive Way of Overhauling Information Systems with SOA

PAPY Fabrice
Information Science

RIVARD François, ABOU HARB Georges, MERET Philippe
The Transverse Information System

ROCHE Stéphane, CARON Claude
Organizational Facets of GIS

VENTRE Daniel
Information Warfare

2008

SMALL BRUGNOT Gérard
Spatial Management of Risks

SMALL FINKE Gerd
Operations Research and Networks

SMALL GUERMOND Yves
Modeling Process in Geography

SMALL KANEVSKI Michael
Advanced Mapping of Environmental Data

SMALL MANOUVRIER Bernard, SMALL LAURENT Ménard
Application Integration: EAI, B2B, BPM and SOA

SMALL PAPY Fabrice
Digital Libraries

2007

SMALL DOBESCH Hartwig, SMALL DUMOLARD Pierre, SMALL DYRAS Izabela
Spatial Interpolation for Climate Data

SMALL SANDERS Lena
Models in Spatial Analysis

2006

SMALL CLIQUET Gérard
Geomarketing

SMALL CORNIOU Jean-Pierre
Looking Back and Going Forward in IT

SMALL DEVILLERS Rodolphe, SMALL JEANSOULIN Robert
Fundamentals of Spatial Data Quality

Lightning Source UK Ltd.
Milton Keynes UK
UKHW021212080120
356541UK00003B/94/P